W9-BDA-881

Barbara Pym

Twayne's English Authors Series

Kinley E. Roby, Editor

Northeastern University

TEAS 406

BARBARA PYM
Painting by Gloria Watts
By the kind permission
of Mrs. Watts.

Barbara Pym

By Jane Nardin

University of Wisconsin—Milwaukee

Twayne Publishers • Boston

Barbara Pym

Jane Nardin

Copyright © 1985 by G. K. Hall & Company
All Rights Reserved
Published by Twayne Publishers
A Division of G. K. Hall & Company
70 Lincoln Street
Boston, Massachusetts 02111

Book Production by Lyda Kuth
Book Design by Barbara Anderson

Printed on permanent/durable acid-free
paper and bound in the United States of
America.

Library of Congress Cataloging in Publication Data

Nardin, Jane, 1944–
  Barbara Pym.

  (Twayne's English authors series; TEAS 406)
  Bibliography: p. 151
  Includes index.
  1. Pym, Barbara—Criticism and interpretation.
I. Title. II. Series.
PR6066.Y58Z79 1985   823'.914   85–774
ISBN 0–8057–6897–1

For John Goulet

Contents

About the Author

Jane Nardin is an associate professor of English at the University of Wisconsin-Milwaukee, where she has been teaching the English novel since 1973. She has published a book, *Those Elegant Decorums: The Concept of Propriety in Jane Austen's Novels,* and several articles on Jane Austen, as well as articles on Samuel Richardson, Anthony Trollope, Henry James, and Evelyn Waugh.

Preface

Only twice during the present century has an English novelist's work, after a period of thorough eclipse, been rediscovered and widely acclaimed for its literary excellence. The two novelists who have enjoyed—or suffered—this fate are Jean Rhys and Barbara Pym, both deceptively unpretentious artists whose books, though in very different ways, center on the concerns of women. What role these characteristics of their work played in breaking and then remaking their literary reputations is an interesting matter for speculation, but unfortunately it cannot be considered here. This preface is concerned only with one practical consequence of the fact that from 1961 to 1977 Barbara Pym's work was almost completely ignored by public and critics alike: the Pym revival has not yet had time to generate, as it certainly will, a substantial body of critical literature concerning her fiction. No book-length study of Pym's novels has yet appeared, and only a few brief articles are at present in print.

Because so little criticism of Pym's fiction has yet been published, I have tried in this study to provide a comprehensive guide that will illuminate the most fundamental issues of theme and technique her work raises. I begin by discussing Pym's life and her use of "autobiographical elements" in her fiction, then try to identify the qualities that make her novels unique and to describe some of her characteristic themes and the way her view of them evolved in the course of her writing career. The remainder of the book contains brief readings of eight novels—the first five and the last three she wrote. I have discussed Pym's remaining two novels only in the introductory chapters, because I find them markedly inferior to her other works. *No Fond Return of Love* has a cumbersome and artificial plot, more like the plot of a stage comedy than like that of other Pym novels, a plot that requires the book's quiet, proper heroine to act in ways that seem to me unconvincing and out of character. And *An Unsuitable Attachment,* though fun to read, clearly lacks both conflict and direction. Written at the close of a decade of great literary productivity, these two novels seem the products of a tired imagination and suggest that the period of hesitation and reappraisal through which Pym passed after *An Unsuitable Attachment* failed to find a publisher may well have had a salutary effect on her uniformly excellent later work. Because I believe that *No Fond Return of Love* and *An Unsuitable Attachment* will not be read or taught as widely as Pym's other books, I have chosen to devote most of the limited space at my command to the eight novels that are now in the process of finding the lasting appreciation they thoroughly deserve.

JANE NARDIN

University of Wisconsin—Milwaukee

Acknowledgments

I am grateful to Hilary Walton, Hazel Holt, and Philip Larkin for sharing with me their memories of Barbara Pym. I also want to thank the Bodleian Library for allowing me access to the Pym manuscripts in its collection, and the University of Wisconsin-Milwaukee for providing a travel grant that helped finance my trip to Oxford to read them. Frank Campenni, John Goulet, Joseph Guerinot, and Tania Modleski read the manuscript and discussed Pym's work with me at what may well have seemed tedious length. Thanks also go to Rachel and Sophia Nardin for taking an interest in Pym's novels; to Gloria Watts for providing the frontispiece; and to Lori Spredeman for typing the manuscript. And I am grateful to Terry Nardin for his readiness to help me in any way he could.

Chronology

1974   Retires from International African Institute to live
       with her sister near Oxford; begins unsuccessfully
       to submit *Quartet in Autumn* for publication.

1977   Mentioned by both Lord David Cecil and Philip
       Larkin in the *Times Literary Supplement* as the most
       underrated writer of the past seventy-five years;
       Quartet in Autumn accepted and published.

1978   *The Sweet Dove Died.*

1979   Completes *A Few Green Leaves.*

1980   Dies on 11 January; *A Few Green Leaves.*

1982   Revised version of *An Unsuitable Attachment.*

Chapter One
Life and Work

Though Barbara Pym's novels are clearly fiction, and not fictionalized autobiography, if one looks for it, one can find in them a great deal of information about her life: the places where she lived, the sort of people she met, her interests, her activities, the ways she changed with the passage of time. "I prefer to write about the kind of things I have experienced and to put into my novels the kind of details that amuse me," Pym once wrote, and the key words here are the words "kind of."[1] Pym does not put her own experiences directly into her fiction, but, because she is a writer whose effects depend upon her sharp eye for the tiny yet revealing detail, she must draw upon places, people, and feelings that she knows intimately to create the world, at once comic and realistic, that characterizes her novels. Indeed, the literary notebooks that she kept for many years show that she frequently observed a detail or scene in her daily round, and then worked it into the novel she was writing at the time. And so Pym's life and novels are linked in complex ways.

Barbara Mary Crampton Pym, the daughter of a prosperous solicitor, was born on 2 June 1913, in the small country town of Oswestry, Shropshire, on the borders of Wales. Pym had one younger sister, Hilary, with whom she was to remain intimate throughout her life. When she was twelve, Pym's parents sent her to Huyton College, a boarding school near Liverpool. Already interested in literature, she was contributing regularly to the school magazine when in 1929 she discovered Aldous Huxley's *Crome Yellow,* which more than anything she had read earlier made her certain she wanted to write novels. Under the influence of *Crome Yellow* the sixteen-year-old Pym wrote a novel that she later described as being "about a group of young 'Bohemians' . . . who were, in my view, young men living in Chelsea, a district of which I knew nothing at the time."[2] Drawing largely on imagination, "Young Men in Fancy Dress" shared little with Pym's mature style beyond a certain wryness and interest in detail.

At eighteen, Pym entered St. Hilda's College, Oxford, and read for her degree in English language and literature, developing an enduring love for English poetry, which was later to be reflected in her novels. Oxford was a perfect environment for romance and friendship, as well as for study, Pym found, and she pursued all three vigorously until taking her BA, with second-class honors, in 1934. Her family did not feel she had to become self-supporting at that point, so she was able to spend the next few years living mostly at home, reading widely and drafting various novels that had more in common with her mature work than did "Young Men in Fancy Dress." Among the writers whom she discovered in the twenties and thirties, and who were to provide more useful models for her later novels than Huxley, were Elizabeth, of *Elizabeth and Her German Garden,* whose wit, irony, and "dry, unsentimental treatment of the relationship between men and women" appealed to her; John Betjeman, whom she liked for his "glorifying of ordinary things and buildings and his subtle appreciation of different kinds of churches and churchmanship"; and Ivy Compton-Burnett, whose most attractive feature was her "precise, formal conversation."[3] And, as Pym herself later remarked, "of course I had also been reading the classics, especially Jane Austen and Trollope. . . . I tend to write about the same kind of people and society they did, although . . . the ones I write about live in the twentieth century. But what novelist of today would *dare* to *claim* she was influenced by such masters of our craft. Certainly all who read and love Jane Austen may *try* to write with the same economy of language, even try to look at their characters with the same kind of detachment, but that is as far as any 'influence' could go."[4]

Only one of the manuscripts that Pym worked on in the thirties survived. Shortly after leaving Oxford, Pym told her sister, Hilary, that she was writing a novel in which she and Hilary appear as two middle-aged women sharing a cottage in a small village—this book, rejected by Jonathan Cape upon its completion, was to be published by the same firm as *Some Tame Gazelle* nearly fifteen years later, in 1950. In the final version of this novel, Barbara Pym becomes Belinda Bede, the rather dim and proper older sister who remembers only scraps of culture from her Oxford days, and Hilary becomes Harriet Bede, the flamboyant, overweight younger sister, whose classical education has disappeared almost without a trace. Though the novel comically projects Barbara and Hilary's personalities thirty years into the future, Pym did not in any way attempt to write a futuristic novel. *Some Tame Gazelle* is an accurate portrait of country life in the thirties, and, though it purports to be a picture of the Pym sisters' middle age, it really tells us about their youth: village life and the role of the parish church in it, Oxford days, and the peculiarities of various Oxford friends who appear as minor characters.

When World War II began, Pym left home to work in the Postal and Telegraph Censorship in Bristol. In 1943, she joined the Women's Royal Naval Service which, toward the end of the war, sent her to Italy for a year. In late 1945, Pym returned to England and rented a flat in Pimlico, a shabby London neighborhood. During this period she was working on a revision of *Some Tame Gazelle,* but with her demobilization in January 1946, it became necessary for her to find a job. Soon she was hired by an anthropological foundation, the International African Institute, as a research assistant. She continued to work for the Institute until her retirement, becoming the assistant editor of its journal, *Africa,* in 1958.

The first fifteen years Pym worked at the International African Institute were the most productive of her literary career. Even before the publication of *Some Tame Gazelle,* she was working on a new book, *Excellent Women,* which would be published in 1952. A more mature and characteristic novel than *Some Tame Gazelle, Excellent Women* paints a detailed and attractive portrait of the London neighborhood in which Pym was living when she wrote it. The heroine, Mildred Lathbury, is, like Pym herself at the time, a spinster in her thirties, from a sheltered background and interested in church affairs, who had worked as a postal censor during the war. One important male character, Rocky Napier—Pym's novels rarely have heroes in the conventional sense—is a recently demobilized Naval officer whose wartime service in Italy consisted of making himself agreeable to Wren officers wearing ill-fitting white uniforms; another, Everard

Bone, is an anthropologist specializing in African tribes and associated with a learned society closely resembling the African Institute.

Excellent Women attracted a positive critical response, but Pym did not wait for its publication to begin work on her next novel, *Jane and Prudence* (1953). The two heroines of this immensely funny book both have something of their author in them. Jane Cleveland is an observant, humorous, imaginative woman with a passion, like Pym's own, for relating her experiences to the seventeenth-century poetry she studied at Oxford. Prudence Bates, selfish, affected, and vain, hardly resembles the quietly humorous Barbara Pym in character, but does share with her a preference for unsatisfactory love affairs over the stability and dullness of marriage. Further, both Jane and Prudence are, like the fortyish woman who wrote the novel, trying to come to terms with the end of their youth and the suspicion that their characters, for good or ill, are formed and can no longer be radically altered.

Pym's next two novels, *Less Than Angels* (1955) and *A Glass of Blessings* (1958), also use some autobiographical material. The former deals with a circle of anthropologists like those with whom Pym had been working at the African Institute, and contains a minor character, Esther Clovis, the secretary of an anthropological organization who, like her creator, takes a kindly interest in the careers of young anthropologists. *Less Than Angels* also asks a question that had begun to interest Pym a good deal after she went to work for the African Institute, a question that a character in one of her later novels ultimately puts into words: "Haven't the novelist and the anthropologist more in common than some people think?"[5] Of this first attempt at a sort of academic novel, Pym later wrote that she felt she "was breaking new ground by venturing into the academic scene, although in many ways that isn't unlike the worlds of the village and parish I'd written about up to then."[6] *A Glass of Blessings* leaves academia and returns once more to the parish—its heroine, Wilmet Forsyth, shares Pym's lifelong interest in church affairs. And Wilmet also shares with Pym the fact that she is an ex-wren officer remembering her days in Italy a decade earlier as a lost period of romantic excitement.

In 1961 Pym published *No Fond Return of Love,* the last and least interesting of her early books. Like all her previous novels, *No Fond Return of Love* was published by Cape, but in 1963, when Pym sent the manuscript of her new novel *An Unsuitable Attachment* to Cape, it was rejected. When an author has published six novels, critically well received and commanding a modest, but loyal public, with one press, and that press flatly rejects a seventh book of the same sort, it is something of an insult—and so Pym felt it. *An Unsuitable Attachment* is another of Pym's novels centering on the church and its most distinctive feature is that it makes greater use of her love for cats than does any of her other books. It was by no means her strongest manuscript, but this was probably not the only reason Cape rejected it. Public taste had turned away from the sort of quiet, realistic comic novel that Pym wrote so well, as the rejection of *An Unsuitable Attachment* by one publisher after another was soon to prove. Writing rather angrily to a friend at Faber and Faber to protest their rejection of the book, Philip Larkin put it this way: "I feel it is a great shame if ordinary sane novels about ordinary sane people doing ordinary sane things can't find a publisher these days. This is the tradition of Austen and Trollope, and I refuse to believe that no one wants its successors today. Why should I have to choose between spy rubbish, science fiction rubbish . . . or dope-taking nervous-break-down rubbish?"[7] Pym herself saw the problem in similar terms. At the end of 1963, she wrote in one of her literary notebooks, "1963 so far. A year of violence, death, and blows," and went on to list some of the blows she had sustained: "My novel rejected by Cape. . . . Reading *The Naked Lunch*. . . . My novel rejected by Heath. . . . *Tropic of Cancer* by Henry Miller (60,000 [?]) copies sold on first day of publication."[8]

After Faber and Faber rejected *An Unsuitable Attachment*, Pym concluded that "probably nothing I write could be acceptable now,"[9] but she continued writing nonetheless. The manuscript on which she was working, with diminished speed and confidence, during the mid-1960s was finished in 1968, but was not to be published as *The Sweet Dove Died* until ten years later. This book probably does represent something of an attempt on Pym's part to adapt her style to the taste of the age, for it deals with a narcissistic, neurotic woman, Leonora Eyre, who lives in a London turned cold and heartless. Leonora's unhappy

relationship with James Boyce, a young homosexual, draws upon
Pym's recent experience of a similar friendship. *The Sweet Dove
Died* is the first of Pym's novels in which the church does not
play a significant role and is by far the most explicit in its treatment of sex—the only one of Pym's books in which destructive
lust is a force to be reckoned with. Some of this shift in tone
is almost certainly due to Pym's desire to please the public,
but more must be attributed to her bitterness at what had happened to *An Unsuitable Attachment* and to her distaste for many
changes that had occurred in English society during the sixties.
Pym altered her tone in *The Sweet Dove Died* and produced an
excellent, if not quite characteristic, novel. But neither its cyni-
cism nor its excellence was sufficient to find it a publisher. As
press after press rejected the book, Pym wrote in her literary
notebook, "What is the future for my kind of writing. What
can my notebooks contain except the usual kinds of bits and
pieces that can never (?) now be worked into fiction? Perhaps
in retirement and even in the year before, a quieter, narrower
kind of life can be worked out and adopted."[10]

In 1974, Pym retired from the International African Institute
and went to share a cottage with her sister in Finstock, a small
village near Oxford. She had been operated on for cancer in
1971, and this experience found its way into *Quartet in Autumn,*
the novel that she now, "with no real hope of getting it
published"[11] and purely for her own satisfaction, began to draft.
Through the character of the terminally ill Marcia Ivory, Pym
turns observations about doctors and social workers that she
made during her own illness into superb fiction. And through
the character of the stoic Letty Crowe, who, like Pym herself
when she wrote the novel, is a woman in her early sixties,
she explores the experience of growing old.

At the end of *Quartet in Autumn,* Letty decides that even
her highly restricted life may still hold "possibilities for
change,"[12] and ironically these words turned out to apply to
Pym herself, sure though she was when she wrote them that
her career as a novelist was over. In 1977, the *Times Literary
Supplement* celebrated seventy-five years of publication by asking
a group of literary figures to list the most underrated writers
of that period, and Pym was the only writer to be mentioned
twice. Both Philip Larkin and Lord David Cecil spoke of her
work in warmly complimentary terms and as a result of these

two important public tributes, interest in Pym's books quickly and dramatically revived. *Quartet in Autumn* and *The Sweet Dove Died* were published by Macmillan in 1977 and 1978 respectively. With recovered spirits, Pym began to work on what was to be her last novel, *A Few Green Leaves.* This novel deals with life in a small Oxfordshire village, similar to Finstock where the Pym sisters were living, in the late seventies. It reflects Pym's continued interest in the church and in the connections between anthropology and literature, as well as newly developed interests in doctor-patient relationships and in local history. *A Few Green Leaves* was finished only two months before Pym's death in January 1980, and her diaries make it clear that she knew she was dying as she wrote it. Its tone is a mixture of wistfulness and cheer, perhaps reflecting her own feelings at the time, and several characters from the earlier books—including Miss Clovis of *Less Than Angels,* who as we have seen had something in common with Pym herself—die in the course of the book. Because Pym often either reintroduces or mentions characters from her earlier novels in her later ones, the whole series creates a sense of continuity like that of a human life— and *A Few Green Leaves,* by drawing together themes and characters from previous works, certainly seems to conclude the series.

Rarely has a writer charted the process of her own death with the stoic calm, the undiminished humor, and the unclouded vision with which Pym describes the recurrence of her cancer in her literary notebooks: "Friday to Dr. Simpson at 10:15. He told me about the pace maker that could be fitted to the heart, but which must be removed at death as it is liable to explode in the crematorium (He said I could put that in a book)."[13] After receiving some devastating news about her condition, she asks wryly, "? Will the cabinet declare a state of emergency tomorrow!"[14] A stay in an intensive care unit, where men lie at one end of the ward and women at the other, reminds her "of Donne—Difference of sex no more we know / Than our guardian angels do. Presumably that might be the intensive care unit."[15] Unfortunately, it isn't practicable to write a novel based on one's own experience of the last stages of a terminal disease, but Barbara Pym, indefatigable observer of life's smallest and oddest details, had taken notes—a practicing novelist to the very end.

Chapter Two

Tradition and Innovation

Barbara Pym in a Literary Context

As one reads Barbara Pym's ten novels for the first time, one is apt to experience them as a curious mixture of the familiar and the strange. The reader will certainly be reminded of Jane Austen by their quiet but often hilarious comedy, avoidance of dramatic and startling events, unerring eye for social detail, focus upon the everyday lives of rather well-off English people, modest, lucid language, and firm, though often unstressed, reliance on a Christian scheme of moral values. And Pym's novels also have some obvious similarities to Anthony Trollope's: their use of the chronicle form, interest in the lives and loves of middle-aged people, skeptical attitude toward marriage, and recurring concern with the varieties of Anglicanism. Clearly, then, Pym's novels revive a great and familiar literary tradition.

But the mere act of transferring the realistic tradition of Austen and Trollope to a mid- or late twentieth-century setting has the effect of radically altering its impact upon readers. We are willing enough, for example, to accept the reality of an early nineteenth-century spinster, like Miss Bates in *Emma,* who contents herself with a quiet life spent in the bosom of her family, but similar characters from Pym's novels, such as Belinda and Harriet Bede in *Some Tame Gazelle* or Rhoda Wellcome in *Less Than Angels,* tend to strike us as anachronisms, in need of special explanation. If they don't marry, why don't they work? If they neither marry nor work, how can they be happy? These days this is the sort of attitude toward the female psyche that we almost automatically espouse. Because she is a twentieth-century novelist Pym's failure to share these attitudes seems somewhat startling.

Other aspects of her work, too, are more surprising in a contemporary writer than they would have been in an earlier era, and confirm the view that Pym is, in some ways, a displaced nineteenth- or even eighteenth-century writer. Though her works certainly do deal with sex, there is little overt sexual activity beyond kisses and embraces in her novels—certainly none that is explicity described, something of an oddity nowadays. Also missing from Pym's novels is the probing of the psyche's murkier areas that twentieth-century readers, more than their eighteenth- or nineteenth-century counterparts, have come to expect. The narrator and the patterning of details in each novel tell us more about many of Pym's characters than they know about themselves, but there are areas of the mind, especially those involving sexual or religious emotion, that Pym does not choose to probe too deeply. The unconscious mind is of little interest to her—as also are questions of social justice, so important in English and American literature from the mid-nineteenth century onward. Even those of Pym's characters who have to earn a living appear to have as much money as they really need, and questions of class come up only as they affect relationships between individuals and are frequently used for humorous purposes.

Nor is Pym's style likely to be quite what the reader of contemporary fiction expects. Her language is simple; her contentment with the conventions of an old-fashioned realism complete; her stories are told chronologically; her handling of point of view makes no attempt at innovation. Two of Pym's novels use simple first-person narration—in one case the narrator is quite reliable, in the other unreliable in a straightforward, correctable way. Her other eight novels employ a flexible semiomniscient third-person narrator who, like Austen's narrators, moves with ease into and out of the viewpoints of various characters.

Readers of Barbara Pym may find themselves wondering how in the almost complete absence of the sexual revelations, the probing of the unconscious, the formal and stylistic experimentation, and the criticism of a basically unjust social, and even cosmic, order, which we expect in contemporary literature, her novels can maintain pace and emotional tension so unfalteringly from beginning to end? How do her books avoid seeming dated by their refusal to follow contemporary norms? The answer is that though she works, as all good artists must, within a tradition, and an old-fashioned tradition at that, Barbara Pym is a highly

original writer, creating a world that is no mere copy of Austen's
or Trollope's. The degree to which she fails to follow the conventions of modernity is not the mark of irrelevance, but of indi-
viduality. Pym rejected the fashions of her era with great
determination and paid, as we saw in chapter 1, a high price
for her resistance. She chose her literary models deliberately,
and adapted them to suit the altered world of which she wrote.

The "Unachieving Character"

Perhaps the most unusual features of Pym's novels are the
sort of people she chooses to write about and the unfailing
respect and sympathy with which she treats them. As one of
the characters in *Quartet in Autumn* complains, "the position
of an unmarried, unattached, ageing woman is of no interest
whatsoever to the writer of modern fiction" (3). And not of
all that much interest to the writer of earlier fiction, either,
she might have added, though there are exceptions of whom
Trollope is perhaps the most notable. Pym sets out to redress
this injustice: of her ten novels, nine have as central characters
aging spinsters, ranging from thirty up through the early sixties,
who remain unattached during most or all of the story. Several
of the novels have more than one important spinster character
and others feature aging bachelors, celibate clergymen, widows,
and widowers. Only a few of these characters marry in the
course of the novels in which they appear; a larger number
seem to be possibly, but not definitely, headed for marriage
after the action concludes—and the rest remain single. Only
three of Pym's major characters are married women—two of
these are childless and the other has only one child. When Pym's
characters, married or single, fall in love, their love is often
mild or transient, an emotion of insufficient power to disturb
radically the calm surface of their lives.

Frequently Pym's characters have only one or two emotional
ties of more than the most casual sort, and their lives, so bare
of love and friendship, are seldom filled by interesting or productive work. The married women in Pym's novels don't work
and this, in combination with their remarkable infertility, leaves
them with a great deal of time on their hands. A surprising
number of Pym's spinster characters, too, seem to have sufficient

independent means so that they can work either part-time or not at all. Some of Pym's men and even a few of her working women have what might generally be thought interesting careers, but most of her working heroines have dull, routine office jobs, only a cut above the work of the typists who make the tea. When Letty Crowe and Marcia Ivory leave their jobs in *Quartet in Autumn,* "the (acting) deputy assistant director who had been commanded to make the presentation speech [at their retirement party] wasn't quite sure what it was that [they] did or had done during their working life. The activities of their department seemed to be shrouded in mystery—something to do with records or filing . . . it was evidently 'women's work,' the kind of thing that could easily be replaced by a computer. The most significant thing about it was that nobody was replacing them . . ." (101).

Pym writes about young lovers as well as aging spinsters, members of parliament, professors, clergymen, and successful businessmen, as well as people doing dull office jobs or living on their private means, men as well as women. But in spite of this range, the population of her novels *is* distinctive in its composition. To put it very simply, Pym's characters generally tend to be older, less involved with other people, especially less involved sexually, and tend to have achieved less than the characters of many other novelists. Typically they have not married, had children, formed close emotional ties, felt great passion, or gotten anywhere in the world of work. Nor in many cases do they seem likely to have most of these experiences later on.

I have said that the population of Pym's novels is an unusual one. But it would be easy to exaggerate just how unusual, for there is, of course, a line of development in fiction beginning with realists like Flaubert, continuing with the naturalists, and becoming pervasive in the twentieth century, which focuses, just as Pym does, on the uneventful or unsuccessful lives of ordinary people who find themselves trapped in restrictive environments. The characters of these writers tend to be younger and less financially secure than Pym's characters, but clear similarities certainly exist. James T. Farrell's Studs Lonigan, to give just one example, has even more trouble finding love, productive work, and a suitable marriage than do most of Pym's protagonists. But if the lives of Pym's characters have something in common with the lives of the characters of such novelists as Flaubert, James, or even Dreiser or Farrell, her approach to what we might call the "unachieving character" is extremely fresh, even unprecedented.

Perhaps a comparison with James Joyce's *Dubliners,* a work comparable in the sort of people it deals with, yet very different in its attitude to them, would be helpful in demonstrating the originality of Pym's approach. Like Pym's characters, the Dubliners tend to be imprisoned in dull, unsatisfactory jobs, to be unable to marry or to find happiness in marriage, and to lack close emotional ties. Joyce sees their "empty" lives as almost totally pitiable and regards them as the paralyzed, or to put it another way, the nearly dead, victims of a destructive society. They are suffering, frustrated, and often violent. Only a few of them, at most, are capable of understanding their own plight as Joyce understands it and then only momentarily.

How completely different is Barbara Pym's treatment of people with similar lives, especially in her early novels. Pym approaches even the most unpleasant of her characters with great sympathy, but unlike Joyce's sympathy, hers is almost always the sympathy of an equal, rather than that of a superior. For accompanying this sympathy is genuine respect for the quality of her characters' experience. A surprisingly large proportion of her quiet characters have perceptions about themselves and the world that are truly intriguing, while few of them are ever exposed to the reader's contempt. Even the least active often have interesting insights and even the most comic remain human. Pym's treatment of her characters is distinctive because, unlike so many writers who deal with similar characters, she does not regard their superficially empty lives as really empty or pitiable. Indeed, she sets out to rehabilitate people whose "achievements" in love or work are small, by showing that a human life can be filled, justified, and even made happy in other ways.

Pym's characters are very much alive beneath their quiet exteriors. An elderly woman in *A Few Green Leaves,* who has been advised to "get involved" as a "prescription for the approach of old age," wonders about the meaning of this prescription: "In a sense we were all 'involved,' weren't we, always had been."[1] There are inactive lives, but in Pym's view, no truly uninvolved ones. Where other writers who deal with the inactive often have in mind implicit standards of adult achievement according to which these characters are judged and found wanting, Pym allows the quiet, isolated life its own positive values, values that her novels extensively and persuasively explore. As one of the characters in *Quartet in Autumn* wonders, "might not the experience of 'not having' [a full, active life] be regarded as something with its own validity?" (25). In ways that we will now begin to examine, Pym convinces her readers that the answer to this surprising question is "yes."

Rhoda Wellcome, one of the more important minor characters in *Less Than Angels,* is a woman in her fifties who has done few of the things that women are "normally" expected to do. Unmarried, Rhoda

had always lived very comfortably, keeping house for her parents, living alone for a short time after their deaths, and then coming to live . . . with [her widowed sister, Mabel Swan]. . . . It was a very satisfactory arrangement and Rhoda was not in the least envious of her sister's fuller life, for now that they were both in their fifties there seemed to be very little difference between them. She would perhaps have liked what she called "the experience of marriage," a vague phrase which seemed to cover all those aspects which one didn't talk about, but she would not have liked to have had it with poor Gregory Swan. She was still sometimes faintly interested in men . . . but in what way she hardly knew. She certainly did not think of marriage any more.[2]

Pym suggests a number of unusual ideas in this subtle passage. Rhoda has had and still has sexual impulses, but the fact that she never did much about them does not mean that she is bitter or frustrated. Keeping house for her parents was not a purgatory, but a source of comfort. Nor is she envious of the marriage and motherhood her sister has achieved, for on some level she is aware that her own condition of faint romantic expectancy may well be more exciting than the "marriage to a good dull man" (35) like Gregory Swan, for which her sister settled. Thus the passage at once directly challenges some stereotypes about spinsterhood and establishes our respect for Rhoda's perceptions, couched in comic euphemism though they are.

Because she lives a housebound, financially secure life, Rhoda
has developed some odd preoccupations, which Pym treats more
positively than one might expect. A methodical and efficient
housekeeper, Rhoda, with little to distract her attention from
the household, is almost uncontrollably irritated by deviations
from her own routines and finds Mabel's disorderly habits very
hard to tolerate. After the family is in bed, Rhoda creeps "quietly
downstairs to see if her sister had laid the breakfast satisfactorily.
She saw that Mabel had made an effort, but there were one
or two things missing, the marmalade spoon and the mats for
the coffee; she put right these omissions and returned quietly
to her room" (44). Taking an evening bath, Rhoda "left the
bathroom as she would wish to find it, folding her own towels
and everyone else's in a special way that pleased her. It worried
her a little that [her nephew] Malcolm was not yet in, for he
would spoil the symmetrical arrangment of the towels and might
splash water on the floor, in the way that men did when they
had a bath" (44). Pym is amused by Rhoda's domestic compul-
sions, but instead of taking Rhoda to task for her concern with
such trivia, she admires Rhoda's ability to control her desire
to dominate her environment. "It irritated [Rhoda] to see Mabel
in the kitchen doing things so vaguely and inefficiently. Sometimes it was all she could do not to interfere, but . . . Rhoda
was sensible enough to realise that it was Mabel's house and
she must be allowed to do things as she liked" (35)—and so
she manages to keep silent. Worried that Malcolm may disarrange the towels when he comes home and takes a bath, Rhoda
tries to console herself with the thought that "if he was very
late he might decide not to have one, there was always that"
(44). Rhoda has found ways to live with her compulsive tendencies for which we must admire her, even as we smile.

Rhoda's suburban parochialism also creates comedy. Told that
an anthropologist friend of her niece, Dierdre, has been killed
in Africa, Rhoda says, "Oh, *no* . . . how terrible. By natives?"
and the woman who is telling her the news sees "past Rhoda's
shocked face into her thoughts, the shouting mob of black bodies
brandishing spears, or the sly arrow, tipped with poison for
which there was no known antidote, fired from an overhanging
jungle tree" (237). When Rhoda hears that these dated supposi-
tions are wide of the mark and that the friend was actually

killed as, dressed in native robes, he mingled with the crowd during an election riot, her response is again comically characteristic: "Oh what a mistake. . . . No good can come of lowering oneself like that" (237). But though Rhoda knows little about the world beyond her suburb, her awareness of her own intellectual shortcomings prevents those shortcomings from making her contemptible. Tuning in late to a radio talk on "the betrayal of freedom," which as good citizens they feel they ought to hear, Rhoda and Mabel are mystified as "a torrent of words rushed at them. A man seemed to be talking, at phenomenal speed, about tables and why they did not rise up into the air" (41). Unable to see what this has to do with the betrayal of freedom, Rhoda switches to a more comprehensible program, commenting sadly and guiltily, "I dare say Malcolm and Dierdre might have understood some of it. . . . *We* cannot hope to now" (41). Her awareness of her own limitations and willingness to blame herself for a failure of comprehension for which the speaker's frenetic style must be at least partially responsible lends her utterance, as the narrator sympathetically notes, "a certain tragic dignity" (41).

And within the confines of her own experience, Rhoda's perceptions do have a certain validity. Rhoda likes to spy on her neighbors from behind her lace curtains, but instead of seeing this habit as the disagreeable meddling of a spinster with no interests of her own, Pym views Rhoda's impulse to live in the lives of others as harmless, demonstrating Rhoda's continuing kindly concern with human behavior. "How much more comfortable it sometimes was to observe from a distance, to look down from an upper window, as it were, as the anthropologists did" (256), the narrator comments, giving Rhoda's studies a tinge of academic respectability.

Peering into the garden of her bachelor neighbor, Alaric Lydgate, Rhoda sees Catherine Oliphant, a young friend of her niece, come out of his house and begin cutting rhubarb. "We could have given her some rhubarb. We have plenty. She needn't have troubled Mr. Lydgate," says Mabel. But Rhoda sees it differently: " 'Oh, I don't suppose he would regard it as being any trouble. . . . Besides it might not be quite the same thing as having it from our garden.' This last point, she felt with some complacency, was of a subtlety that perhaps only

an unmarried woman could fully appreciate " (256). Rhoda's
point isn't quite as subtle as she herself thinks it, but she is
indeed the first person in the novel to notice the affection developing between Alaric and Catherine. The spinster who has never
stopped searching for romantic love, and not the woman who
found out where romance leads when she married a good dull
man, has the livelier insight into its nature. The woman with
the limited life is not necessarily a woman with an empty mind.
She has her areas of competence and insight, her moral triumphs,
though she has them in forms so muted, so odd, that few novelists other than Pym would have been interested in asserting
their value or even in demonstrating their existence.

Rhoda's case is typical of the way Pym affirms the dignity
of her dull or inactive characters. Less typical, but in a way
more clearly revealing of Pym's methods is the case of Marcia
Ivory in *Quartet in Autumn*. A fatally ill, quite batty spinster
in her sixties, this retired woman lives what might be called a
secret life in the London house she inherited from her parents.
None of her neighbors, old acquaintances from her working
days, doctors, or even the social worker who frequently visits
her, has the least idea of what Marcia does with her time. With
their conventional, sane approaches to human behavior, they
are able to notice only the normal things that she fails to do:
clearly she does not eat, she is so thin; she does not talk about
herself as most people do; she doesn't clean her house, which
is an unholy mess; she doesn't go out or have visitors. To these
people Marcia's life appears empty, disordered, pitiable, for her
actual activities and interests are so bizarre, so mad, yet so quietly
carried on, that no one except Pym and the reader knows anything about them.

[Every week Marcia] bought some tins for her store cupboard and
now she spent some time arranging them. There was a great deal of
classifying and sorting to be done here; the tins could be arranged
according to size or by types of food—meat, fish, fruit, vegetables,
soup, or miscellaneous. This last category included such unclassifiable
items as tomatoe puree, stuffed vine leaves (this was an impulse buy)
and tapioca pudding. There was work to be done here and Marcia
enjoyed doing it.

Then, as the day was fine, she went into the garden and picked her way over the long uncut grass to the shed where she kept milk bottles. These needed to be checked from time to time and occasionally she even went as far as dusting them. Sometimes she would put out one for the milkman, but she mustn't let the hoard get too low because if there was a national emergency of the kind that seemed so frequent nowadays or even another war, there could well be a shortage of milk bottles. . . . (64)

Marcia's emotional life, like her daily activities, is secret and strange. Her stay in a hospital where she had a mastectomy and particularly Mr. Strong, the surgeon who performed the operation, have evoked a hidden, but powerful, emotional response. Usually ragged, she buys "new pink underwear" (49) for her checkups at Mr. Strong's office, as well as "a drawer full of new . . . nighties—not at all what you'd imagine Miss Ivory wearing judging by the rest of her clothes" (164), for a possible future hospital stay. Her rigid face softens into a smile like that of a young girl in love when she sees anything reminiscent of illness or hospitals. Marcia's interests and emotions are hardly ones that the reader is likely to admire or envy, but Pym's descriptions give them a surprising richness and suggest that, outward appearances notwithstanding, Marcia's life is fascinating in its bizarre way. Unlike Rhoda Wellcome's life, Marcia's cannot be said to reveal hidden values that attract the reader, but it does reveal a hidden order and fullness of its own.

When her ex-coworkers come to clean up Marcia's disastrously filthy house after her death, they immediately acknowledge her peculiar aesthetic achievements, commenting upon the "spotlessly clean," milk bottles, "so beautifully washed and arranged," on the "array of tinned goods . . . so beautifully arranged and classified" (214–15), and even on the "plastic bags of various sizes, all neatly folded and classified by size and type" (199). Though Marcia is by a great deal the most aberrant protagonist in any of Pym's novels, the riches of her secret life can perhaps be seen as emblematic of Pym's general approach to her characters, for it is her usual practice to suggest that beneath the surface of the blankest lives something with its own kind of interest lies concealed. If this is true of Marcia, then clearly it could be true of just about anyone.

It is perhaps possible, in spite of the differences among Pym's quiet characters, to make some generalizations about their sources of satisfaction. The one most universally enjoyed by Pym's protagonists—though not, as it happens, by Marcia—is the joy of minutely observing the activities of others: Pym's own joy, in short. Nearly every Pym novel contains a female "observer" character whose subtle remarks on psychological and social topics delight or instruct the reader and who becomes a spokeswoman for the author. "Virtue is an excellent thing and we should all strive after it, but it can sometimes be a little depressing," says Mildred Lathbury of *Excellent Women.*[3] "Understanding somebody else's filing system is just about as easy as really getting to know another human being. Just when you think you know everything about them, there's the impossible happening, the M for Miscellaneous, when you naturally assumed it would be under something else" (109), Catherine Oliphant remarks in *Less Than Angels.*

It is not, however, entirely because they are naturally intelligent that Pym's observer characters see the world so clearly. In part, at least, their abilities are nurtured by the circumstances of their quiet lives, and therefore it is not surprising that so many of them are women, a point to which we shall return in the next chapter. Often the observer characters possess, as we have seen, a great deal of leisure and rarely are their energies absorbed by a struggle to achieve worldly success. In the absence of many outlets for action, observation becomes their chosen activity, and in most cases proves to be a highly satisfactory one. In *Excellent Women* one of Mildred Lathbury's old friends, William Caldicote, takes her out to lunch. It is William's business, not Mildred's, to order the meal, and as he does so, she sits quiet and unoccupied, watching him and listening: "He was in a fussy mood today, I could see, as he went rather petulantly through the menu. The liver would probably be overdone, the duck not enough done, the weather had been too mild for the celery to be good—it seemed as if there was really nothing we could eat. I sat patiently while William and the waiter consulted in angry whispers. A bottle of wine was brought. William took it up and studied the label suspiciously. I watched apprehensively as he tasted it, for he was one of those men to whom the formality really meant something and he was quite likely to send the bottle back and demand another.

But as he tasted, he relaxed. It was all right, or perhaps not that, but it would do" (67). In this scene, so quintessentially Barbara Pym, the person who "sits patiently" and observes others, rather than the one who acts to achieve the fulfillment of desire, better understands the situation *and* has the better time.

In Pym's novels, characters who do not choose to go after what they want often have yet another source of superiority to the active—the chance to avoid painful collisions between imagination and reality and so to keep the imagination alive. Pym's married women characters are all shown to be wistfully dissatisfied with the sense of closed possibilities, to which their achievement of the married state has brought them. It is perhaps fitting that Rowena Talbott, the character in all Pym's novels who comes closest to having what many people would think of as a full and normal woman's life—marriage to a rich, attractive husband, and three young children to keep her busy—should voice this emotion most clearly. "Sometimes, you know," she tells her married friend Wilmet, "I envy really wicked women, or even despised spinsters—they at least can have their dreams . . . if we do, we know that there's absolutely no hope of their coming true. Whereas the despised spinster still has the chance of meeting somebody. . . . At least she's *free.*"[4] It is no accident, either, that Rowena with her superficially full life is a minor character in *A Glass of Blessings,* while the childless Wilmet, plagued by a sense of uselessness, is the heroine. Rowena's "fulfilled" state doesn't interest Pym very much; Wilmet's "emptiness," and the hidden things that really fill it, do. In the next chapter, we shall consider how Pym's feminism relates to her view of the connection between imagination and reality.

Several of Pym's novels suggest that frustration of desire can sometimes, in its own way, be a pleasurable state of being. "Of course," Belinda Bede in *Some Tame Gazelle* thinks at one point when her ultra-high standards of propriety have prevented her from accepting an invitation, "there was a certain pleasure in not doing something; it was impossible that one's high expectations should be disappointed by the reality. To Belinda's imaginative but contented mind, this seemed a happy state with no emptiness or bitterness about it."[5] Pym wryly expresses a similar sentiment in one of her diaries: "The lunch you didn't have with him will be more wonderful than all the past ones."[6] Many

Pym characters choose to be quiet and undemanding in their
approach to life. The often disappointing reality of satisfied desire is something they rarely have to confront.

"Oh what joy to get a real calf's foot from the butcher and
not have to cheat by putting in gelatine," thinks Catherine Oliphant, as she prepares a classic *boeuf à la mode,* a thought, surely,
that few novelists other than Pym would be likely to put into
a heroine's head. "The small things of life were so much bigger
than the great things, she decided, wondering how many writers
and philosophers had said this before her, the trivial pleasures
like cooking, one's home, little poems, especially sad ones, solitary walks, funny things seen and overheard" (LTA, 104). As
Catherine suspects, this is not a new idea, but Pym gives the
idea reality in unexpected ways, for her novels devote much
space to the seductive depiction of many small pleasures that,
like observation, are at least as available to people who live
quietly as they are to the active and successful. Some of these
pleasures have received little attention from other novelists.

Although Pym seldom describes sexual activity—thus tactfully
implying that perhaps its importance in many people's lives tends
to be exaggerated by contemporary novelists—she is lavish in
her descriptions of food—implying thereby that food as a pleasure, and as a part of the texture of daily life, has not received
its due in the novel. When the anthropologist Emma Howick
sees a group of village women decorating their church for a
flower festival, she wonders, "Was the festival itself in some
way connected with fertility, perhaps? Looking again at the as-
sembled group of ladies, she doubted this interpretation. It was
a mistake to suppose that every activity was related to sex, whatever Freud might say" (AFGL, 77). Pym agrees, but food is
a different matter and really does pervade daily experience.
Scores of meals, many delicious, some comically awful, nearly
all revelatory of the characters of those who cook or eat them,
are minutely described in the course of Pym's ten novels. Indeed
the novels contain, if one cares to look for it, a history of the
changing diet of England from the thirties to the late seventies.

The heroine's day often commences with elaborate menu planning. For Belinda Bede in *Some Tame Gazelle,* one particular
Sunday began "as other Sundays did. After breakfast, Belinda
had consulted with Emily [the maid] about the roast beef, and

together they had decided what time it should be put into the oven and how long it ought to stay there. The vegetables—celery and roast potatoes—were agreed upon, and the pudding—a plum tart—chosen. In addition, the chickens for the supper party were to be put on to boil and Emily was to start making the trifle if she had time" (103). Sometimes food is clearly more seductive than sex. Dining with the handsome Fabian Driver, Prudence Bates is more interested in the meal than in her companion. "The chicken will have that wonderful sauce with it, thought Prudence, looking into Fabian's eyes. She had ordered smoked salmon to begin with and afterwards perhaps she would have some Brie, all creamy and delicious."[7]

Pym is also interested in a pleasure that has perhaps never received much attention from any other novelist: solitary eating. Coming home after a day of work, Prudence Bates "poured herself a gin and French. . . . When she had finished her drink she went to the kitchen and started to prepare her supper. Although she was alone, it was not a meal to be ashamed of. There was a little garlic in the oily salad and the cheese was nicely ripe. The table was laid with all the proper accompaniments and the coffee which followed the meal was not made out of a tin or bottle" (JP, 47). And Pym shows her characters eating, alone and in company, in an entertaining variety of restaurants ranging from sordid cafeterias where one finds oneself "worrying, imagining grit and live things" in the salad (AGB, 23), to the elegant Simpson's "famed for its meat, where great joints were wheeled up to the table for one's choice and approval" (AGB, 88).

Pym also devotes an unusual amount of attention to the pleasure of literature, particularly poetry. Many of Pym's characters—especially, as we shall see in the next chapter, in her early novels—have degrees in English literature from Oxford, or if self-educated like Catherine Oliphant, are still extremely well read in English poetry and fiction, or if not really literary at all, like Mildred Lathbury, find many a quotation to ponder in the Anglican liturgy, hymns, or devotional books. For all these characters the ability to relate their experiences to their reading is a great enrichment of life, though it isn't always done in the most profound manner. After an upsetting evening, Belinda Bede "surprisingly, in a far-away voice," says to her sister

Harriet, " 'I wonder what it would be like to be turned into
a pillar of salt?' 'Belinda!' Harriet exclaimed in astonishment,
'Whatever made you think of that? Potiphar's wife, wasn't it,
in the Old Testament somewhere?' 'I think it was Lot's wife,'
said Belinda, 'but I can't remember why. I should imagine it
would be very restful . . . to have no feelings or emotions' "
(STG, 79–80). The sometimes bittersweet joy of finding an
apt quotation or literary parallel is an important one for Pym's
characters, and one of the few times that the narrator expresses
real pity for a character occurs when she sees that character
missing out on the pleasures of literature. Elaine, in *Less Than
Angels,* has not recovered from her first broken romance because

the circumstances of her daily life, less usual now than fifty or a hundred
years ago, were not conducive to easy forgetting. . . . Elaine had
been the one to stay at home. She might, if she had come upon them,
have copied out Anne Elliot's words, especially as she was the same
age as Miss Austen's heroine: "We certainly do not forget you so
soon as you forget us. It is perhaps our fate, rather than our merit.
. . . We live at home, quiet, confined, and our feelings prey upon
us. You are forced on exertion. . . ." But Elaine was not much of
a reader; she would have said that she had no time, which was perhaps
just as well, even if she missed the consolation and pain of coming
upon her feelings expressed for her in such moving words. (196)

Elaine has missed one wonderful way of filling her quiet life
and expanding her awareness, and though greater awareness
would have brought pain as well as pleasure, the experiences
of many other Pym characters show that the pain is by no means
too dearly purchased. And if the literary allusion does not mingle
pain and pleasure, it can simply be a source of quiet fun. Seeing
a village woman wearing an unusually smart hat, "a maroon
felt with a paste ornament in the form of an anchor," Emma
Howick, remembering "a hymn from schooldays," thinks,
"fierce was the wild billow, dark was the night, Oars laboured
heavily, foam glimmered white" (AFGL, 58) and shares a moment of amusement with the reader.

   After food and literature, clothes and the home rank highest
on Pym's list of quiet pleasures. Some of her heroines are completely uninterested in clothes—Jane Cleveland, for example,

goes about in "an old tweed coat . . . the kind of coat one might have used for feeding the chickens in" (JP, 49)—but more typically they worry about their dowdiness if they feel lacking in style. Clothes are Wilmet Forsyth's passion and she describes many of her outfits, down to the tiniest of accessories: "The only ring I wore . . . was my engagement ring, an eighteenth-century setting of rose diamonds, so much prettier than a modern one" (AGB, 42). In addition, many of Pym's characters are highly domestic, finding such things as well-set tables and well-brushed staircases to be harmless and dependable sources of pleasure.

Catherine Oliphant thinks that life is "comic and sad and indefinite—dull sometimes, but seldom really tragic or deliriously happy, except when one's very young" (LTA, 89). Because Pym agrees, her novels tell of the ordinary daily pleasures and renunciations that are important to all, rather than of the "big" events and emotions that often seem to play less of a role in life than in literature. By building her novels out of a multitude of everyday details and by making those details interesting, Pym convinces her readers that lives lacking dramatic incident, great passion, or great achievement need not be empty lives. And so it is significant that Pym prefers to exclude highly dramatic incidents almost completely from her novels, choosing as material for her plots such small "events" as the way two people whose flats share a common bathroom decide to apportion the cost of their toilet paper. In Pym's novels exciting events either seem to be promised but fail to materialize—Wilmet Forsyth does not have an affair, Rocky and Helena Napier do not get a divorce, Dulcie Mainwaring's fiancé decides not to marry her—or else fail to arouse the expected extreme emotions. When James Boyce in *The Sweet Dove Died* is seduced by a young woman he meets at a party, his main response is an uneasy feeling "that he had behaved most unwisely"[8]—no rapture, certainly. The everyday occurrences that fill Pym's novels seem far more significant than the very occasional dramatic events they describe.

Living as quietly as they do, Pym's protagonists sometimes react with real excitement to the smallest events. At the close of an afternoon during which she has lunched with one friend and called on another, the usually isolated Wilmet Forsyth is left with a feeling that "the day had somehow been too full" (AGB, 167). When Belinda Bede, who has loved Henry Hoccleve fruitlessly for thirty years, is asked to mend a hole in his sock—*on* his foot, no less—she finds it an "upsetting and unnerving experience" (STG, 79), almost more than she can handle.

In these ways Pym builds into the structure and texture of her novels a convincing refutation of the idea that those who never achieve much or experience dramatic events and emotions are bored emotional cripples. She creates a context in which a narrator can remark that a group of aging spinsters taking tea together "were all very gay, in the way that happy, unmarried ladies of middle age often are" (STG, 169), without arousing the surprise that such a view of the aging spinster might be expected to produce. Her readers understand how and why an aging spinster living quietly in a country cottage might be as interesting and, indeed, as contented a person as a married brain surgeon, whose hobbies are mountain climbing and managing a wine chateau in the Gironde.

Not all Pym's characters, to be sure, are as contented as the spinsters of *Some Tame Gazelle,* a novel about middle age written when Pym was in her early twenties and imbued with a level of youthful high spirits that she never quite reached again. At her gloomiest she agrees with Dr. Johnson that there is generally much to be endured and little to be enjoyed in the lives of men. Like Catherine Oliphant, she is well aware that "we are strangers and pilgrims here and must endure the heart's banishment" (LTA, 138), cut off by our fallen nature from completely satisfying intimacy either with other men or with God. But for a Christian of Barbara Pym's sort these are universal truths, applying equally to successful people and to the less successful with whom her novels deal. Experts in endurance and emotional banishment, Pym's quiet characters become more capable of appreciating the small "moments of happiness" (LTA, 154) that life grants to all. We do not merely sympathize with them, we like and admire them as well.

Comedy

However, we laugh at them too. If one of the distinguishing features of Pym's work is her respect for the integrity of her characters, the other is the quality of her humor. Much of the forward momentum that Pym's almost plotless novels maintain so consistently is provided by their comedy, for she is a writer who commands a dazzling variety of comic effects. On occasion, Pym indulges in comedy for its own sake—a minor character will appear briefly and do a comic turn that is so broad as to be almost Dickensian, and that has little connection with the remainder of the novel. Traveling by train, the hero of *No Fond Return of Love* overhears a conversation between a clergyman and his female companion, who are apparently going to a funeral bearing bunches of flowers: " 'The notice in *The Times* distinctly said "cut flowers only," ' the woman remarked. 'Quite—and you picked something out of the garden, mostly leaves as far as I remember,' said the clergyman, with a hint of malice. 'That's far more what poor old Basil himself would have wished,' said the woman firmly. 'A few *natural* flowers—whatever there happened to be in the garden, even if it wasn't very much—rather than an expensive sheaf of *wired* flowers from a Kensington florist. He would have hated the idea of *wired* flowers—he *abhorred* cruelty in *all* its forms. . . .' "[9]

More typically, however, Pym's humor is less broad than this and does not depend upon marked exaggeration for its effect. Because Pym sees so clearly the conflicts of emotion, the repressions, the misunderstandings, the inconsistencies, and the odd juxtapositions that make up the texture of daily life, she can amuse, and even convulse, merely by describing them. She paces and arranges the comic details in her novels with great skill, but the details themselves are generally quiet, even understated. Pym can thus produce wonderful comedy without destroying the highly realistic feeling of her novels. When she chooses to use exaggerated comic effects, she is careful to place them in a context that prevents their extremity from doing violence to the realism of her world. In *A Glass of Blessings,* Wilmet Forsyth, making a donation at a blood center hears a "rather mad looking woman" arguing with the attendants: " 'I really cannot wait in the queue. I am Miss Daunt,' I heard her say in a loud, ringing tone. 'My blood is Rhesus *negative,* the most valuable kind. I have a letter from the Regional Director.' She seemed to fumble with a paper, then raised her voice. *'This precious blood,'* she read, 'that is the phrase used. And you expect me to wait here behind all these people!' " (78). Listening,

Wilmet wonders whether Miss Daunt is completely insane or "only a little odd" (78), and is glad to move away from her as soon as possible. By making it clear that Miss Daunt strikes everyone as an obvious eccentric, Pym can use her for a comic effect (the unintended pun on the "precious blood" of our redeemer) that is exaggerated yet not improbable.

At her comic best, however, Pym uses the most everyday material imaginable. As Jane and Nicholas Cleveland are spending their first evening in their new vicarage, Nicholas notices a visitor walking toward the house and tells Jane "there *is* somebody coming. . . . A lady, or perhaps a woman, in a straw hat with a bird on it, and she is carrying a bloodstained bundle" (JP, 17). The comedy of this line does not come from oddity or exaggeration. In his attempt to describe the visitor, the class-conscious Nicholas naturally considers amending his first descriptive term "lady" to the less socially misleading "woman." But when he refers to her as "perhaps a woman," it sounds for a moment as if he may be uncertain of her sex, or as if he may think that some ladies are not women at all. Nicholas's remark is funny because of these unintentional comic undertones and also because it shows so economically how important categories of class are to the way he views the world. The incongruous detail of the bloodstained bundle—not something one would expect a strange lady, or even woman, to carry when making a formal call in a fancy hat—also turns out to be explicable and normal, for the visitor is the Clevelands' new maid, with some liver for their supper. Because Nicholas's observations of the woman's appearance become more and more minute, until at last he notices even the bloodstains on her bundle, his comic remarks also create a convincing sense that she is walking toward the house as he speaks. Pym's comedy is typically precise and illuminating in just this way.

Pym's favorite comic subjects recur often in her books. One of these is the discrepancy between what people think and what they say. The clergyman, Tom Dagnall, in *A Few Green Leaves,* recalls a "particularly interesting stone" that a clerical diarist whose works he once read had noted finding near the stately house that he and some elderly parish ladies are visiting. But he quickly decides not to mention his further recollection that the stone was described as having "borne a shape closely resembling the female pudenda" (167). Another of Pym's recurrent comic topics—the possibly misleading social implications of London addresses and the way people deal with those implications— might not seem particularly promising material for humor, yet Pym manages to make it work. "The address is 28 Montgomery Square, SW1, but don't let the SW1 deceive you," one character in *An Unsuitable Attachment* says maliciously to another, who is preparing to visit a mutual friend. "It's Pimlico, not Knightsbridge or Belgravia" (108). The selfishness and carefully calculated domestic incompetence of men is another frequent source of humor for Pym. A priest in *A Glass of Blessings* whose housekeeper has just quit adds an "agitated postscript" announcing this disaster to his pastoral letter in the parish magazine: "Now we are *really* in the soup. Prayers, please, and *practical* help. Isn't there some good woman (or man) who would feel drawn to do *really Christian work* and look after Father Bode and myself?" (26). Often Pym's characters are found singing hymns whose words give comic insight into their thoughts. One of the characters in *A Glass of Blessings* invites his female houseguest, in whom he is sexually interested, to slip off with him, ostensibly to visit the local church, and immediately after making this proposition begins to hum "We plough the fields and scatter" (41). Social pretension, selfishness disguised as humility, and the discrepancy between thought and expression are all classic materials for comedy, of course, but in Pym's novels they take characteristically muted forms.

Sometimes Pym uses a running joke to unify a novel. *Jane and Prudence* suggests several variations on the old saw that men want only one thing, with extremely humorous effect. Miss Doggett, a spinster friend of Jane's, quotes this platitude to her, but immediately afterwards appears to be "puzzled; it was as if she had heard that men only wanted one thing, but had forgotten for the moment what it was" (70). On another occasion, Miss Doggett returns to this theme, telling Jane," 'We know that men are not like women . . . you and I, Mrs. Cleveland—well, I am an old woman and you are married, so we can admit honestly what men are.' 'You mean they want only one thing?' said Jane. 'Well, yes, that is it. We know what it is' " (127). But again Miss Doggett fails to specify. Still later, Miss Doggett is telling Jane about the odd sermons preached

by the former missionary who replaced Nicholas while the
Clevelands were on vacation: " 'We got very tired of Africa
and I didn't feel that what he told us rang quite true. He said
that one African chief had had a thousand wives. I found that
a little difficult to believe.' 'Well, we know what men are,' said
Jane casually, surprised that Miss Doggett, with her insistence
on men only wanting one thing, should have found it difficult
to believe' " (213).

Pym frequently makes comic capital out of oddities and incon-
gruities of feeling and behavior of which her characters themselves are not fully aware. But in other cases it is a character,
especially a major character, and not the narrator, who is the
source of the wonderfully observed humorous detail that delights the reader. For Pym's "observer" characters often have
a keen eye for the funny, as well as the serious, details of everyday life, and an admirable self-critical sense. Remembering how
when she was at Oxford her future husband Nicholas used to
come to visit her on his bicycle, Jane Cleveland also recalls
that at the time she did not dream "that he was to become a
clergyman—though, seeing him in the hall with his bicycle clips
still on, perhaps she should have realised that he was bound
to be a curate one day" (13). Here Jane sees, as Pym does,
the comic overtones of the well observed detail: Nicholas is
so innocent about the sexual implications of dress that he doesn't
think to remove his absurd-looking bicycle clips before entering
his girlfriend's presence. But at the time Jane herself was so
innocent that she failed to note the significance of this detail,
as she now realizes. In this way Pym uses her comedy to increase
the reader's respect for the quality of her characters' perceptions.

Patterning

Pym does not usually order the multitude of small but interesting details out of which her novels are constructed so as to
make relatively unambiguous thematic points of the sort that
are, for example, Jane Austen's or George Eliot's stock in trade.
Most of Pym's novels are indeed organized around thematic
concerns, some of the most typical of which will be discussed
in the next chapter, but they treat their themes in a manner
that is peculiarly their own and that harmonizes well with their

rejection of the striking and dramatic in the areas of character and plot. Pym's basic strategy in dealing with theme is to tantalize the reader by refusing to complete the patterning of her details. This tendency is more marked in some novels, for example *Less Than Angels* and *Jane and Prudence,* than it is in others, such as *Some Tame Gazelle* and *A Few Green Leaves,* but typically Pym looks at both sides of a theme and refuses to commit herself wholly to either. Leonora Eyre, in *The Sweet Dove Died* is so egotistical that she rejects the one human being she truly loves because he has been guilty of temporary disloyalty to her—a humiliation she simply cannot forgive. Though readers are made fully aware of Leonora's selfishness and her inability to accept love's necessary compromises, they cannot condemn her because they must also realize that in making her decision to avoid the indignities love sometimes forces people to undergo by avoiding love itself, she has acted on a sound understanding of her own character. Thus Pym's thematic complexity and the sympathy she is able to feel for her most unpleasant characters go hand in hand. For Pym there is no right or normal way to live, only a multitude of more or less peculiar accommodations between nature and circumstance, which her novels with generous tolerance explore.

It may sound odd to say that for a Christian writer like Pym there is no ultimate answer to any of life's largest questions, yet this surely is the case. Pym is committed to Christian morality in general, but the details of belief concerning which Christians disagree don't seem to interest her very much. Toleration and forgiveness are the aspects of Christian ethics she stresses. Her most likable characters, always aware of human mortality and imperfection, strive to be charitable and humble in their dealings with others. When there is trouble in his parish, Nicholas Cleveland tells his wife, " 'We must accept people as we find them and do the best we can.' . . . in too casual a tone to sound priggish" (JP, 138). Asked to prohibit tasteless monuments in the graveyard of his church, Tom Dagnall asks how he can "act in . . . a high-handed and unfeeling manner towards fellow human beings at a time of sadness, still suffering the grief of bereavement? After all, everybody couldn't be blessed with the gift of good taste . . . unpalatable as it was to acknowledge a common humanity with those who would cover their graves

with green marble chips" (AFGL, 104). Clearly this is Pym's
attitude to her characters as well: accepting the imperfection
of all, she denies her sympathy to none.

But where theological questions are concerned it is much
more difficult to attribute opinions to Pym, or for that matter
to her characters. Many of her characters do go to church regularly, pray, and think about God, yet a sense of uncertainty
seems to plague them and the reader isn't certain either about
what they believe. During a meeting of her husband's Parochial
Church Council, Jane Cleveland tried "very hard to realise the
Presence of God in the vicarage drawing room but failed as
usual, hearing through the silence only Mrs. Glaze running water
in the back kitchen to wash up the supper things" (JP, 133).
Does she never succeed in feeling God's presence, then? And
what of Rupert Stonebird, in *An Unsuitable Attachment,* a clergyman's son who suddenly regains his lost faith during an impulsive
visit to the parish church near a house he is planning to buy?
"It had been an uncomfortable and disturbing sensation," the
narrator comments rather surprisingly, "he had almost considered not buying the house, but . . . how was he to know that
things would be different in another district" (35). What sort
of faith *is* it that Rupert has found, if he contemplates fleeing
in an attempt to recover his atheism? Pym doesn't say.

Some of Pym's characters seem to value the church primarily
for the stability it provides. Thinking of the traditional rhythms
of the church year, Edwin Braithwaite in *Quartet in Autumn* is
pleased to conclude that "that was how it always had been and
how it would go on in spite of trendy clergy trying to introduce
so-called up to date forms of worship, rock and roll and guitars
and discussions about the Third World instead of evensong"
(74). For Pym the spiritual life is a mystery that she will not
try seriously to penetrate; Christian faith is a way of organizing
one's life and of approaching the frightening questions raised
by being alive. Faith takes a different form for every Christian
individual.

There are no final answers to any of the questions we want
to ask about life, because life teases us with patterns that invariably remain incomplete, unsatisfactory. Taking tea in a restaurant, Catherine Oliphant looks through the window and notices
two anthropologists of her acquaintance walking in the opposite

direction from the stream of rush-hour pedestrian traffic. "Where could they be going at this time, in the wrong direction? Catherine wondered. Was it perhaps significant that two anthropologists, whose business it was to study behavior in human societies, should find themselves pushing against the stream? She hardly knew how to follow up her observation and made no attempt to do so, only asking herself again where they could be going" (LTA, 8). The narrator knows where they are going, but Pym declines to answer Catherine's more general question about anthropologists definitively. Some of the anthropologists in her novels are highly conventional, while others do appear to view their culture critically and to push against its stream in one way or another—there is no clear pattern, no answer.

On some occasions, indeed, the way Pym suggests a pattern and then refuses to define its meaning can be quite maddening. The two heroines of *Quartet in Autumn,* Marcia Ivory and Letty Crowe, have surnames that certainly suggest that the novel will make use of some sort of dark / light, good / evil pattern of symbolic detail. And other details that seem possibly related to such a pattern do in fact appear, clustered especially around the figure of Marcia. Marcia's dyed dark brown hair grows out, becoming first piebald, then white, in the course of the novel. Her cat, Snowy, had spots of black fur that faded before his death, and even worse, when Marcia tries to exhume his body, she can't locate it. Since Marcia, too, dies at the end of the story and since her death draws the story's other protagonists closer together, one might be tempted to see these details as saying something of a religious nature about redemption through suffering. But it is finally impossible to make the details fit this hypothesis.

Potentially significant thematic patterns are often only partly defined in Pym's novels, and the symbolic overtones of individual details are frequently puzzling as well. At the end of *Jane and Prudence,* Fabian Driver and Jane are talking in her conservatory about his complicated love affairs, when she notices "the headless body of a [stone] dwarf which had once stood in the rockery in the front garden" lying near them and feels an impulse to offer it to him "as a kind of comment on the futility of earthly love" (214–15). There is enough that is symbolically suggestive about the broken dwarf to make us sympathize with

Jane's desire to see it as a symbol for the emotionally incomplete
Fabian or for defective humanity in general, yet it isn't a symbol
of "the futility of earthly love" in any clear way. Looking into
Alaric Lydgate's garden, Rhoda Wellcome sees him "in the
vegetable part at the back, apparently digging up potatoes. . . .
Ordinary actions, perhaps . . . but . . . it seemed as if they
must have some strange significance" (LTA, 175).

   Pym's characters are thwarted in their desire to find the symbolic significance that ordinary events and objects sometimes
hint at, and her novels often raise and then frustrate this desire
in her readers as well. Again and again the detail that we want
to see as symbolic refuses to oblige. Leonora Eyre is certainly
not an exemplar of deep fidelity like Beethoven's Leonora, and
in her beauty and emotional coldness she is the opposite of
Jane Eyre, whom her name also suggests. The widow, Mrs.
Crampton, and the novelist, Barbara Bird, in *Jane and Prudence*
and the typist, Miss Pim, in *A Glass of Blessings,* have names
that imply some connection with their creator, Barbara Mary
Crampton Pym, but the nature of the connection is puzzling
to the ordinary reader, though here we may have allusions that
make more sense to readers who knew Pym personally. By
frustrating our desire for order and significance in these obvious
ways, Pym calls attention both to that desire and to the artificial-
ity with which many novelists try to satisfy it.

   Pym's approach to the psychology of her characters also leaves
room for large areas of mystery. Just as she presents details
with the utmost clarity, but refuses to fit them into completely
controlled thematic patterns, so too she holds that human beings
can know a lot *about* one another, but can never really *know*
one another. "Who does know anyone?" a character in *Quartet
in Autumn* asks uncomfortably. Pym can define her characters'
nature very precisely within certain limits and yet beyond those
limits leave uncharted territories of psychic mystery. Frequently
her narrators qualify their analyses of human motives with a
"perhaps," or offer alternative explanations of them. Fabian
Driver's extramarital affairs are described with this sort of indefi-
niteness: he "seemed to need [them] either to bolster up his
self-respect or for some more obvious reason" (JP, 57).

   And there are areas of human motivation that Pym apparently
finds irreducibly mysterious. The spiritual life, as we have al-

ready seen, is one of these; sex is another. What exactly is the nature of the "faint stirring of interest" Marcia Ivory feels at one time for her coworker Norman, "a feeling that was a good many degrees cooler than tenderness, but which nevertheless occupied her thoughts briefly" (23)? And why, at her funeral, is Norman "strangely disturbed by the idea of Marcia lying in her coffin. . . . He didn't know whether to laugh, which you could hardly do here, or cry, which you couldn't do either" (188). Is this passage about Norman's fear of death, his repressed sexuality, or both? What gives his thoughts their tinge of hysteria? In her refusal to complete either her patterns or her explanations of her characters' minds, Pym shows that, her links to earlier novelists notwithstanding, she is a twentieth-century writer after all.

Pym's distinctive endings also contribute to the sense of life's irresolvable complexity which her novels as a whole create. At the end of *Some Tame Gazelle,* Belinda Bede, certain that she will never marry, contemplates with pleasure a future— exactly like the past—in which she "would continue to find such consolation as she needed in our greater English poets, when she was not gardening or making vests for the poor in Pimlico" (250–51). Wilmet Forsyth, once dissatisfied with her idle existence, decides at the close of *A Glass of Blessings* that her life is really full enough. When *Excellent Women* concludes, Mildred Lathbury appears headed for a marriage that will not change her life dramatically, as also does Catherine Oliphant, at the end of *Less Than Angels.* Emma Howick, of *A Few Green Leaves,* will apparently make a marriage based on tastes and desires that she has always had but never understood, a marriage that therefore represents an accommodation with her own nature, rather than a change in it. The dual heroines of *Jane and Prudence* and Leonora Eyre all come to realize that they must accept themselves and their lives, with all the attendant shortcomings, more or less as they are. Only in *No Fond Return of Love* and *An Unsuitable Attachment* do the conclusions give a sense of dramatic, significant change. Both Dulcie Mainwaring in the former novel and Ianthe Broome in the second make unexpected romantic marriages that will truly alter the texture of their daily lives.

So in most of Pym's novels, and even for some of the charac-

ters in the last two mentioned, there are endings, but no conclusions. The characters have been living uneventfully, almost
secretly, and in many cases contentedly, and the interest of the
novels has come from the sense Pym gives of the texture of
their daily lives and thoughts, rather than from their involvement
in dramatic situations or even from what their activities can
tell us about "large," significant themes. Whereas the tiniest
actions in Jane Austen's novels are significant precisely because
they are clues to very important social or moral issues—when,
for example, Lydia Bennet in *Pride and Prejudice* spends her
lunch money on a new bonnet, leaving her sisters to pay for
the meal, the reader is justified in concluding that she lacks
prudence, has no sense of moral obligation, and is likely to
get into serious trouble—the tiny details in Pym's novels tend
to be significant in different ways. Of course they always illustrate
character, but they need not, and often do not, provide clues
to life's larger issues, for they are themselves the stuff of life
and as such have their own baffling sort of significance. "It's
the trivial things that matter, isn't it?" (AGB, 87) says one of
Pym's characters, and Pym agrees. If larger thematic issues are
raised through these details they often are not completely re-
solved and the characters must simply continue the business
of daily living when the novel's last page is reached, with few
of their questions answered.

So it is appropriate that the novels often seem to end rather
arbitrarily and abruptly, in a way that is likely to take the reader
by surprise. Because of the open quality of their endings, Pym's
novels can use the chronicle form—in which characters from
earlier novels reappear or are mentioned in later ones—without
creating a sense that the integrity of perfect, symmetrically pat-
terned works of art has been violated. We know from the way
each book ends that its characters will go on struggling with
the irresolvable problems of everyday life, and we are not at
all surprised to learn from the later books that they are indeed
doing so. Pym's novels, seemingly so old-fashioned in their subject matter and form, in fact use innovatively understated approaches to character, humor, plot, theme, symbolism, and
resolution to make their readers understand that ordinary lives,
when closely and sympathetically scrutinized, may turn out not
to be so ordinary after all. If we approach the novels searching

for highly dramatic events and issues we will fail to find them, but we may decide we can do without them, as Pym shows us that the ordinary, the quiet, and the incompletely defined can provide the basis for a satisfying portrayal of human life.

In chapters 4 and 5, which analyze individual novels, we will be mainly concerned to trace the most significant patterns those novels suggest, but it should be remembered that doing so may well create the impression that the novels are more rigidly controlled by pattern and theme than is in fact the case. The patterns we shall be looking at in those chapters are important, but in all Pym's novels texture and a sense of life's complexity and paradox are at least equally important—and far more difficult to discuss and define.

Chapter Three

Thematic Development

Certain aspects of human experience continued to fascinate Pym throughout her writing career, and her last three books reexamine ideas, character types, settings, and situations that had figured prominently in her earlier work. Like *Jane and Prudence, The Sweet Dove Died* deals with a beautiful, narcissistic woman and contrasts her emotional state with that of women who, less vain, are more able to love. *A Few Green Leaves* returns to the village setting Pym used in *Some Tame Gazelle,* but thematically it revisits the territory of *Less Than Angels* and takes a fresh look at the relationship between social science and literature. *Quartet in Autumn* resembles *Some Tame Gazelle* in dealing with a group of unmarried people in late middle-age who must come to terms with their loneliness. That a writer like Pym, who hesitates to offer final answers to the questions she raises, should wish to return and reexamine those questions seems natural enough—but perhaps she had another motive as well. Because of the hiatus in her publishing career, Pym's reuse of material from an early novel in a late one allows her to examine the changes that had occurred in England during the intervening period. In general, Pym did not find these social changes appealing, and her last novels are therefore darker in tone, grimmer in their handling of the issues they raise, and more critical of English society than were her earlier books. In this chapter, I shall discuss three of the themes that interested Pym and briefly trace her changing view of England between the mid-1930s, when she drafted *Some Tame Gazelle,* and 1979, when she finished *A Few Green Leaves.*

Love

One of the subjects that continued to fascinate Pym is love, and as we might expect from her tolerance and willingness to explore the eccentrically winding byways of the human heart, her novels do not either explicitly or implicitly articulate a standard of "adult sexual love" to which her characters are expected to conform, though the articulation of such a standard is a fairly common occurrence in modern fiction. Because Pym concentrates on love's odder manifestations and suggests that sexual love often fails to be as central to their lives as people expect, her approach implies that one should not take a restrictive view of love's nature.

Some Tame Gazelle, Pym's first novel, is rather uncharacteristic of her work in the insistence with which it asserts the absolute need for "something to love, oh, something to love," in virtually all its characters. The novel is, however, pure Pym in its examination of the surprising ways in which this need can be fulfilled. Belinda Bede, the heroine, is satisfied to lavish her love on Henry Hoccleve, her college sweetheart who married another woman thirty years before. Her fidelity to Henry warms Belinda's heart even though she cannot hope for a return to her affection. Belinda's sister, Harriet, finds her emotional sustenance in a series of handsome young curates, for whom she knits socks and makes jam with a kind of fierce, but impersonal, affection. For each of these women the quality of her relationship with the object of her love is unimportant—they come close to obeying Elizabeth Barrett Browning's injunction to love for love's sake only. The characters here must love *something* and for that reason they may choose very peculiar objects for their devotion.

Though none of Pym's later novels makes this point in the emphatic manner of *Some Tame Gazelle,* many of them do use characters whose need to love is satisfied by a relationship that, though stable, is unconnected with marriage, or indeed with any kind of sexuality. Some characters, like Daisy and Edwin Pettigrew in *An Unsuitable Attachment,* love animals to the exclusion of people. Edwin's wife, in fact, left him because their marriage needed "more of himself than he could spare from the animals" (24). Others, like Edwin Braithwaite of *Quartet in Autumn,* love an institution. And so Edwin's passion for "the dear old C of E" (24) led him to leave his wife to her own devices "for long evenings when [he] was at meetings of the parochial church council" (184). Still others love one person exclusively, but nonsexually, as Meg in *The Sweet Dove Died* loves her young friend Colin, who is for her a surrogate child. Several live with siblings who seem to be fully as important to them as a spouse might be.

Indeed, many of Pym's novels suggest that love need not play a more central or satisfying role in the lives of married people than it does in the lives of single ones. Mildred Lathbury, who was never "very much given to falling in love" (EW, 44) develops a crush on a charming married man, Rocky Napier, and discovers how much suffering love can cause. She recovers from her infatuation, however, and at the end of the novel appears to be moving toward marriage with a man who doesn't awaken a very powerful emotional or sexual response in her, but who needs a sensible, helpful wife. Mildred has decided that she either can, or must, get along without passionate love— service to others and mild affection will take its place at the heart of her life. It is *Excellent Women's* central irony that marriage will not bring Mildred the sort of love or "fulfillment" any spinster need envy.

Pym's married women protagonists, too, discover after marriage what Mildred figured out beforehand: that romantic love "is only one of many passions and it has no great influence on the sum of life," as a character in *Some Tame Gazelle* is "fond of quoting" (144). If they are as intelligent as Jane Cleveland, this insight may cause them no problems, and may even arouse some wistful amusement: "Mild, kindly looks and spectacles, thought Jane; this was what it all came to in the end. The passion of those early days, the fragments of Donne and Marvell . . . all these faded away into mild, kindly looks and spectacles. There came a day when one didn't quote poetry to one's husband any more" (JP, 48). But for less self-aware women the loss of romance in marriage can be quite a blow. Wilmet Forsyth's thoughts stray to other men, while Sophia Ainger, not really happy with her self-sufficient husband, Mark—"he's not of this world, you know" (AUA, 99)—still compulsively, if vicariously, pursues romance as she tries to find a husband for her younger sister. At its best, marriage provides these women with a cozy companionship that, though pleasant, *can't* quite be the center, the justification for their lives. Thus, ironically, the odd passions for cats or high church services become more important to Pym's characters than "normal" married affection.

In the novels that follow *Some Tame Gazelle,* Pym also develops an interest in characters who are unable to love with stability or fidelity, and she treats them with surprising gentleness. Some characters' ability to make a commitment to anything outside themselves seems to have been destroyed by the possession of great beauty or charm, an accident of birth for which they cannot be blamed. Thinking of handsome Fabian Driver's rather theatrical wretchedness at having to reject one of his numerous girl-friends, Jane Cleveland reflects that "presumably attractive men and probably women too must always be suffering in this way; they must so often have to reject and cast aside love" (JP, 192). The "suffering" that comes from having to reject devotion is surely the most pleasant kind of suffering imaginable; no wonder that so many of Pym's characters become addicted to it, finding admiration and the excitement of transient love affairs more delightful than stable, long-term devotion. Where other women make marriage or a career the emotional center of their lives, Prudence Bates " 'has her love affairs' . . . they were surely as much an occupation as anything else" (JP, 10). The transient feelings these characters have for others are just a manifestation of their exaggerated self-love. But Pym suggests they may adjust quite comfortably to their situations—flattery simply taking the place of commitment in their lives.

In Pym's later novels characters begin to appear who for reasons of nature or circumstance have not developed the ability to love. "In the past . . . Letty . . . might have loved or been loved," the narrator of *Quartet in Autumn* remarks, but because her fate never realized this possibility, in Letty's old age "the feeling that should have been directed towards husband, lover, child, or even grandchild, had no natural outlet; no cat, dog, no bird, even, shared [her] life" (10). Unable, now, to feel passion for anything, Letty is nonetheless a decent, kindly woman and quite heroic in the brave way she bears her loneliness.

Men vs. Women

In the world of Pym's novels, where men are greatly outnumbered by women, the former seek success and the realization of their own desires through doing the sort of work that society rewards, while the latter suppress their own desires and devote themselves to caring for others. Considering that many of Pym's novels were written in the late forties and the fifties when such insights were severely out of fashion, she gives her tart reflections on the exploitative relationship of men to women surprising prominence. But even more surprising than the fact that Pym has these feminist insights is what she chooses to do with them. Instead of taking the common feminist position that women must seek equal opportunity to realize their own desires, Pym's novels suggest that it is in fact men, rather than women, who are the main victims of sex role differentiation.

"Women like me really expected very little—nothing, almost" (EW, 37), thinks Mildred Lathbury, whose life is not made "meaningful," either by the traditional female achievements of marriage and children, *or* by the substitute achievement that many feminists would recommend, interesting work. From both the traditional male and the usual feminist point of view, Mildred is a victim who has "almost nothing," but for Pym she has almost everything, precisely because her world has given her so little. Quiet, withdrawn, cautious, and unassertive, Mildred is not, however, the stereotypical intuitive, irrational woman. She has the traditional feminine interests in religion and personal relationships, but she sees her world with the cool, detached accuracy of an outsider who has plenty of leisure for observation. And because she knows that she *is* an outsider in the "significant" affairs of her society, condescendingly treated by many with whom she comes in contact, Mildred has developed the self-irony that also characterizes women in Pym's novels. Her isolation and obscurity have fostered the mental independence that allows her to question the value of many activities that social "insiders" automatically assume to be worthwhile. Pym suggests that the interests, abilities, and freedom of reflection that Mildred shares with many of her other female characters are in and of themselves sufficient to justify and fill her life. She does not have to use her abilities in order to make or achieve anything—her life is justified by what she sees, by her possession of a woman's heightened consciousness.

Unlike many of the female observer characters in her novels, however, Pym was not content to view observation wholly as an end in itself, but wanted to turn her observations of the world around her into fictional artifacts of lasting value—a contradiction that may suggest that she was more oriented toward achievement than she permits her most likable characters to be. But perhaps this is less contradictory than it seems. The fact that Pym went on jotting down observations in her notebooks and producing novels during the fifteen years when she felt fairly certain that what she was writing would never see the light of day suggests that, like her heroines, she found satisfaction in observing and in shaping her observations for herself alone. And, indeed, a few of her heroines are interested, as she was, in giving some sort of permanent form to what they observe. But for both Pym and her protagonists observation has a value whether one writes it down or not. The desire to create something *from* what one observes remains secondary to and quite separable from the pleasure and value of observation itself.

The lives of Pym's male characters are made less valuable by the fact that they frequently have not developed the kind of consciousness that distinguishes her women. Conditioned to want and expect worldly success, even if only of so mild a sort as success in the ministry, Pym's men tend to lack the ironic distance from their own pursuits that makes her women so attractive. Rarely are Pym's women characters professors, doctors, business executives, or successful civil servants—and obviously they are never ministers. Even the most achieving of them tend to be engaged in "feminine" activities that neither their society, nor they themselves, take completely seriously. Catherine Oliphant is humorously aware that the romantic fiction for women that she writes isn't "serious" literature: for her audience "life itself was sometimes too strong and raw and must be made palatable by fancy, as tough meat may be made tender by mincing" (LTA, 7). The articles she produces for women's magazines are also a matter for humor: "Having dealt with the problem of acquiring a good suntan and then bleaching away its last traces, she was now thinking of winter beauty treatments, getting the arms and shoulders nice for new year parties, softening those rough elbows. Try sitting with your elbows cupped in halves of lemon, she thought derisively, advice she would never have dreamed of following herself" (194).

A woman is often forced to take this approach to her work, but Pym's men frequently view theirs without any irony at all, even though what they accomplish is by no means certain to be more valuable than, for example, the imaginative consolations of Catherine's work are to her readers. Many of Pym's male characters are absorbed by their work, accepting the standards and the jargon of their professions uncritically, even eagerly, losing distance, losing their ability to observe the world around them freely or spontaneously. "Prior to the commencement of my second field trip" (111), writes Catherine's anthropologist friend Tom in his Ph.D. thesis, and when she suggests "some simplification of this phrase" (112), he fails to see what she has in mind, so completely has he internalized the ghastly stylistic standards of his respected profession. There is much reason for Tom to view his work ironically, but little in his environment encourages him to do so. Even Pym's clergymen—who tend to be the nicest males in her novels, and whose jobs, as we shall see later, in some ways really do promote humility—are often made egotistical by the admiration they receive, or uncritically employ the solemn rhetoric that is their stock in trade. At a moment of tension, even a decent clergyman like Julian Malory of *Excellent Women* can do this, becoming "pompous and clerical, almost like a stage clergyman, his voice taking on an unctuous quality which it did not usually possess. 'She worships at St. Mary's. . . . The other morning after I had said Mass'. . . his conversation seemed stilted and unnatural" (159).

Conditioned to go after what they want, to act rather than to observe, to think of themselves rather than of others, to exercise authority rather than to evade it, Pym's male characters rarely develop the sort of consciousness so many of her women possess. Pym never uses a male as her main point-of-view character, and indeed chooses only a few times to use a man as one of a group of point-of-view characters. And the reason for this is clear: a man's consciousness is not usually developed so as to serve as the primary source of the minute observations of daily life that are the stuff of Pym's novels. Men are interested in "larger" things. When Tom Dagnall walks into a friend's house and looks around, the narrator comments that, of course, "he did not take in as much detail as a woman would have done" (AFGL, 91)—and yet Tom is clearly one of the most sensitive men in Pym's novels. Given the values that those novels so persuasively recommend, this failure to note the significant detail is serious and outweighs the achievements in terms of which men are superior to women.

Deprivation and perhaps also freedom from the necessity to succeed in a career produce feminine morality as well as feminine consciousness. Women's necessarily self-effacing, quiet lives have often been seen as causally related to their moral excellence, and Pym agrees, though with some interesting reservations. That a woman should be the center of attention seems unnatural to the inhabitants of the male-centered society Pym depicts. A man in *A Glass of Blessings* wonders "whether it would really be proper to admit women to Holy Orders. Is it likely that a woman would be surrounded by men" as the clergy are always surrounded by women at parish gatherings, "and would it be seemly if she were?" (207). Leaving the meeting of a literary society, Jane Cleveland, taking a last look round, sees "one woman rendering homage to a poet and another mopping spilt coffee from the trousers of a critic," and comments, "things like that aren't as trivial as you might think" (JP, 120). No, indeed, for the end result of all the deference and homage men receive is egotism and selfishness.

Pym's men typically expect a lot of attention from women. In *A Few Green Leaves,* Graham Pettifer asks Emma Howick, an ex-mistress of his into whose neighborhood he is moving, to order some groceries to be ready for his arrival. After performing this hospitable chore, Emma visits Graham and receives, not thanks for the favor, but complaints about the quality of the food. "I found the groceries—rather an odd selection. . . . It seemed odd to have tinned vegetables in the country—I'd imagined produce from people's gardens, even yours. And I don't *much* care for spaghetti hoops. . . . Oh, and there was a loaf of *sliced* bread. . . . I was hoping you'd come last night— bring something you'd cooked yourself" (131–32). Having delivered himself of these complaints, Graham breaks off the conversation, telling Emma, "I must work in the mornings" (132). Clearly Emma has the moral advantage here and this scene, though a bit extreme, does reflect the way Pym usually treats male and female moral development. An even more dramatic example of this appears in an unpublished novel of academic shenanigans, which Pym was writing during the sixties. Alan, a lecturer, asks his wife, Caro, to steal a manuscript from the

room of an elderly, bedridden academic—once prominent in
Alan's field—to whom Caro has been paying visits as an act
of charity![1] In this case, the way career pressures help to shape
male character is particularly clear.

Graham, Alan, and many of the other men in Pym's novels
use their work as a justification both for carefully calculated
domestic incompetence and for selfishness. "I had observed,"
remarks Mildred Lathbury sharply, "that men did not usually
do things unless they liked doing them" (EW, 9). If women
want to control their own lives in this way—and sometimes
they do—they must resort to traditional feminine ploys like
hypochondria, as Bertha Burdon does in *An Unsuitable Attachment* when she says, "I *have* to eat meat, unfortunately—doctor's
orders" (93), as a reason for failing to fast during Lent. Or
they must dominate those weaker than themselves—and in
Pym's novels this usually means another woman—as Miss Lee
bosses her female companion in *A Few Green Leaves.* Pym's world
doesn't allow women the scope for the expression of selfishness
that it allows men.

Pym's views on the subject of men and women are among
the most consistent in her work, yet even here the matter is
more complex than it initially seems. If "enforced" failure, inactivity, and self-suppression produce feminine decency, as well
as feminine awareness, there may be men whose lives or tem-
peraments have simulated these conditions and who therefore
resemble women in various important respects. Because this
happens fairly often in Pym's novels, they do not seem excessively hostile to men. A man like Rupert Stonebird in *An Unsuitable Attachment,* who is temperamentally timid and unassertive, may well feel so uneasy about his lack of masculinity as
to view his own behavior with the same kind of ironic distance
that characterizes feminine consciousness in Pym's books. Talking to a young woman on the telephone, Rupert is unable to
nerve himself to make an overture. "Ask her out to dinner,
he told himself, but somehow he could not get the words out
and then the line started to crackle as if it were a long distance
call over oceans and continents" (208). The ironic tone of the
last clause here suggests that Rupert knows he is merely rational-
izing his fears when he attributes his loss of courage to the
crackling line—the sort of amusingly self-critical insight Pym

usually reserves for women. Knowing what it feels like to be at a loss, Rupert develops an "uncomfortable conscience" (206) toward the sufferings of others, which also connects him with Pym's women. For these reasons, Pym is able to use Rupert as one of several point-of-view characters in *An Unsuitable Attachment.*

Rupert develops something of a feminine consciousness because of his constitutional timidity, but in his relationship to his work as an anthropologist he is a typical Pym male, hiding "himself away in the Vatican Library to work—a natural but perhaps slightly cowardly thing for a man to do" (185), when his personal affairs become uncomfortably complex, and generally using his professional success as a crutch to prop his personal insecurity. Suggestively, "his study, with its big, untidy desk strewn with folders of notes and the proofs of a book he was correcting, was to him the most congenial room in the house," while his dining room, the room of hospitality and socializing, "faces north and is difficult to heat" (119).

Other male characters, however, are often "feminized" by failure. Piers Longridge in *A Glass of Blessings* has failed at a variety of occupations—"sometime this, formerly the other" (45) is the general drift of his resumé—and so has acquired a sense of his own weakness and dependence on the help of others that Pym usually reserves for women. "Aren't we all colleagues, in a sense, in this grim business of getting through life as best we can?" (198), he asks sadly at one point. Piers also lacks the vocational self-definition that makes so many of Pym's male characters a bit tedious. "Teaching is creative work . . . you must feel that you are molding people," says Piers's sister, trying to cheer him up about the evening classes he teaches by suggesting that he is doing important work, as a man should. But Piers replies with gloomy honesty, "You should see what I have to mold" (50). Piers has an ironic distance from his own pursuits that Pym's successful men can't match. Very young men, who have not yet been fully absorbed into a profession, and retired men, who have passed the stage at which professional identity means everything to them, may also escape some of the worst consequences of being male.

And if Pym is concerned to qualify her basically unenthusiastic view of men, she is no less concerned to bring into balance her admiration for a certain sort of quiet, self-sacrificing woman, for such women can play a crucial role in spoiling men. Walking through London, Catherine Oliphant, usually no churchgoer, enters a strange church to say a prayer. While praying, she hears people approaching and fears they will "ask her what she was doing there. But the voices, when they came, were women's voices, and the snatch of conversation she heard was not really very alarming, showing as it did the universal concern of women for men: '. . . will wear himself out. If only he would let Father Amis take the early Mass sometimes. The trouble is that one can do so *little* oneself, one feels so helpless' [says the voice Catherine hears]. Two middle aged women came out of a door, one of them carrying a small electric bowl fire" (LTA, 196).

The humility and kindness of the woman speaker who carries the ambiguously suggestive torch are placed in a less positive light when Catherine encounters Father Summerhayes, the supposedly overworked cleric, as she leaves the church. "Hullo, Miss Dewsbury. . . . Still keeping up the good work?" (196), he calls out, mistaking Catherine for one of his numerous female helpers who are clearly too unimportant to be remembered individually. Catherine imagines herself as an excellent woman "worrying over Father Summerhayes," but can't get far with the idea because she immediately realizes that in fact the priest "had not . . . looked at all worn out" (197). The habits of detached observation and the habits of self-sacrifice, which are both products of the way women live, can finally take them in opposite directions.

And Pym prefers the women in whom powers of humility do not take precedence over powers of observation. Her novels contain many women whose lack of respect for themselves, excessive deference to men, and almost automatic self-criticism make them comic. The most attractive characters counterbalance feminine humility by feminine consciousness. "Ah, you ladies! Always on the spot when things are happening!" an acquaintance tells Mildred Lathbury, with typical male contempt for a spinster's trivial pursuits, when he meets her as she watches some furniture being moved into the flat below her own. His "roguish tone made me start," comments Mildred, showing the equally typical female tendency to accept blame for just about anything.

But Mildred immediately realizes that a guilty start in this particular situation implies that "I had no right to be discovered
outside my own front door" (EW, 5), clearly an absurd idea—
and so she turns the tables on her smug and unreasonable critic.
The only real beneficiaries of the quietly, but dramatically, sexist
culture Pym's novels portray are the women characters who,
like their creator, can see men as they are. Men themselves,
as well as the women who have internalized this society's view
of their own inferiority, are its victims.

Religion, Literature, and Science

If we find a man in one of Pym's novels blaming himself
when he is not in the wrong, or indeed even when he *is*, he
will probably turn out to be a clergyman. A high proportion
of the men in Pym's books are either clergymen or academics,
especially anthropologists. And this introduces us to the third
of Pym's recurrent thematic concerns: the opposition between
religious or literary and scientific or social scientific modes of
viewing the world. Religion, literature, and science are, in a
sense, simply different ways of approaching the same question:
what does it mean to be a human being in society and in the
universe? And there is no reason that these approaches need
be mutually exclusive.

In a biographical talk called "Finding a Voice," which she
made for the BBC in 1978, Pym credited the familiarity with
anthropological methods that she acquired in her work for the
International African Institute with helping her develop her distinctive style: "I learned how it was possible and even essential
to cultivate an attitude of detachment towards life and people,
and how the novelist could even do field work as the anthropologist did."[2] Pym's precision, balance, and unwillingness to raise
extreme emotions or judge her characters harshly do indeed
have much in common with the anthropologist's approach to
his material.

But though there are complex links among religion, literature,
and science, there is also one basic opposition between religious
and literary approaches to human experience, on the one hand,
and social scientific approaches on the other. Neither religion
nor literature claims that even under the most ideal circum-

stances it could provide complete and objectively true answers to the questions it considers, whereas the social sciences do sometimes claim to be working toward such explanations of human behavior. It is because they are well aware that they can provide visions of reality that have only a subjective, imaginative sort of truth, that literary artists are so willing to "rush in with their analyses of the heart and mind and soul of which they often have far less knowledge than [an anthropologist] has of his tribe" (LTA, 167). And anthropologists must be more careful precisely because they claim objective validity for their conclusions. They will typically oppose cautions like "it would, however, be dangerous at this stage to embark on any extensive analysis" (LTA, 167) to the poet's or novelist's bold willingness to reach for an imaginative truth that can never quite be grasped. When the anthropologist Tom Mallow attends a flower festival in his home village, "the scene reminded him of the African festivals he used to attend, observing meticulously how this or that old custom . . . had died out and been replaced by some new and 'significant' feature, avoiding in his descriptions the least suggestion of vivid or picturesque language" (LTA, 177). Tom mistakes literary flatness for scientific validity.

As Pym sees it, religion resembles literature rather than social science in the small degree of certainty it claims for its attempts to make sense of life. As we noted in the previous chapter, Christianity for Pym offers guidance, not answers, and of course acknowledgment of life's mystery is central to Christianity. "God moves in a mysterious way his wonders to perform," "Thy way, not mine, O Lord," and similar lines from well-known hymns are often quoted in Pym's novels, stressing the idea that Christianity cannot clear up all our perplexities and that those perplexities will continue to trouble us until, at death, we put off our blindnesses along with our bodies.

This basic difference between literary or religious and scientific approaches to experience means that, in Pym's novels, people who approach life through religion or literature tend to be more decent and humble than scientists, for they are generally aware that they have no direct pipeline to truth, no privileged knowledge denied to ordinary people. This can be most clearly seen in *A Few Green Leaves,* which of all Pym's works draws the sharpest distinctions between scientific and religious views of experience.

His education in medicine and psychology have convinced the young doctor Martin Shrubsole that he knows what is true and good for his family and patients in every area of life. Martin is quick with a diagnosis that places him in a position of superiority, deciding, for instance, that Miss Vereker, one of those terrifyingly sane, self-disciplined, and stoic elderly women that Pym occasionally portrays, is "in need of psychiatric help" (224), simply because his first meeting with her occurs under rather odd circumstances that make him suspect her motives. No charitable suspension of judgment occurs, for Martin is sure he's right—after all, he is a trained psychologist. In prescribing a "scientific" diet for his mother-in-law, Martin moves with equal assurance and equal confusion about his own motives: "Magdalen Raven was . . . inclined to be overweight, though Martin had succeeded in 'weaning' her away from sugar in tea and coffee, so that she now carried saccharine pellets in her handbag. . . . In this way Martin was fulfilling his duty as a conscientious general practitioner. . . . But he did sometimes wonder whether he really wanted to preserve his mother-in-law all that much. . . . This thought, instantly stifled, had more than once occurred to Martin. . . . But, of course, after it had occurred, he became even more conscientious in the preservation of his mother-in-law. . . . 'Couldn't you try taking tea or coffee without any sweetener?' he had suggested" (52–53). Unaware that the hostility toward his mother-in-law, about which he feels so guilty that he cannot openly admit its existence, helps motivate his desire to deprive her of her few remaining pleasures, Martin continues to prescribe for her with complete confidence, sure all the weight of science is behind his pronouncements. Social scientists in Pym's novels usually lack the direct power over others that a doctor possesses, but they tend toward similar arrogance.

The nature of a clergyman's work, on the other hand, encourages him to fix his attention on man's fallen nature, the "humanity in which we all share" (QA, 206), and to be tolerant, forgiving, and humble before life's mysteries. After attending the funeral of an acquaintance, Emma Howick in *A Few Green Leaves* learns from the clergyman Tom Dagnall, who is Martin Shrubsole's opposite number, that "it was customary for the mourners to be present in church on the Sunday after the funeral. These particular people would not be seen at a service again until the next funeral, marriage, or christening" (233). When Emma expresses indignation at the way the mourners use the church only when it suits them to do so, ignoring it at ordinary times, "Tom, in his kinder and more tolerant way, pointed out that it gave a kind of continuity to village life, like the seasons— the cutting and harvesting of the crops, then the new sowing and the springing up again" (233). Tom can see the behavior of the mourners, which is not personally flattering to him, in a larger context. Human life is cyclical and the church plays a part in its cycles, even for people who are not enthusiastic about religion. Being a humble and tolerant man with a clear sense of the imperfection of all earthly things, Tom is quite content with this small consolation.

But not all of Pym's clergymen are as completely decent as Tom, who is a good man by nature as well as by his Christian convictions, and who enjoys one additional advantage over many of Pym's other clerical characters. Because he lives at a time when religion has become unfashionable, Tom has been spared the most dramatic effects of the spoiling to which Pym's clergy- men are often subjected by those crowds of "excellent women," unattached and ready to idolize their parish priests, who frequent Anglican churches in the early novels. When, in *Less Than Angels,* Father Tulliver goes to dinner at the house of his parishioners, Rhoda Wellcome and Mabel Swan, the talk turns to missions. " 'Oddly enough,' [Father Tulliver] said thoughtfully, as if it were a matter of surprise to him or even a kind of oversight on somebody's part, 'I have not had the call to the Mission Field. I have felt, wrongly perhaps . . . that my work lay here.' 'Oh, you couldn't leave us, Father, not when you've got every- thing so nice, the services and all that,' said Rhoda" (148), and later she returns to the subject again, imploring Father Tul- liver flatteringly, "I do hope you *won't* go to the Mission Field, Father" (150). Since Father Tulliver hasn't the slightest inten- tion of leaving his comfortable suburban parish to labor in the bush, Rhoda's concern is comic, but it's easy to see how a steady diet of this sort of flattery, along with hand-knitted socks, scarves, and pullovers, homemade jam, and cakes brought to the door, might well counterbalance the effects of Christian teaching and produce a clergyman who was anything but humble.

In addition, there is no real reason to expect Christians, or even clergymen, to be better than other people. "Churchgoers are used to being accused of things. I have never found out exactly what it is that we do or are supposed to do," says Mildred Lathbury, when her neighbor Helena Napier makes a spiteful reference to "these so-called good people who go to church." " 'We are whited sepulchres,' said Everard [Bone, also a churchgoer, in reply]. 'We don't practice what we preach. Isn't that it, Helena?' 'One expects you to behave better than other people,' said Helena, 'and of course you don't.' 'Why should we? We are only human, aren't we, Miss Lathbury?' " Everard sensibly points out (EW, 97). Because Christians believe that human imperfection is ineradicable, they are not very troubled when their fellow believers are unable to practice what they preach.

And since each believer develops his or her own particular brand of Christianity, it should cause no surprise that in Pym's novels unpleasant people often make unpleasant Christians, or even clerics. Pym's novels contain many clergymen whose temperamental unfitness for their role is only partially corrected by the lessons it is their duty to teach. Comfort-loving aesthetes, like Father Thames and Father Ransome in *A Glass of Blessings,* devote unsuitable amounts of time and money to "amassing Fabergé eggs and Dresden china" (111). Other priests, like David Lydell in *Quartet in Autumn,* are constitutionally uncharitable, and still others, like Neville Forbes in *No Fond Return of Love,* are naturally flirtatious, or naturally cold, like Mark Ainger in *An Unsuitable Attachment.* Only when the proper temperament combines with Christian teaching do we get such exemplary clerics as the kindly and modest Father Bode, of *A Glass of Blessings,* who, discussing his chances of being appointed rector in a parish that he desperately wants, is able to say, "of course the Bishop could so easily find a better man," and to say it "so sincerely that it sounded as if he really meant it" (184).

A Changing England

It is largely because Pym feels as she does about religion, literature, and the social sciences that the novels she wrote after *An Unsuitable Attachment* failed to find a publisher in 1963 are darker in tone than her earlier works. If we compare these two groups of novels, we see that the late novels tend to portray a world in which social units are becoming larger and less manageable, in which social science is replacing both literature and religion as the preferred way of apprehending experience, and in which love and companionship are becoming rarer and manifesting themselves in less satisfactory forms.

The first difference between the world of Pym's first seven novels and the world of her last three is a loss of community. *Some Tame Gazelle* is set in a tiny village where the inhabitants constantly meet, observe one another's activities from behind their curtains, and pick up information about each other from the servants' grapevine. When Agatha Hoccleve, the archdeacon's wife goes on vacation, "Belinda and Harriet had been at their posts by the window for about ten minutes before there was any sign of life at the vicarage. . . . To watch anyone coming or going in the village was a real delight to them, so they had looked forward to this morning with an almost childish excitement. . . . What would Agatha wear? Would she have a great deal of luggage or just a suitcase and a hat-box? Would the Archdeacon go with her to the station in the taxi?" (70–71). Years of this intense scrutiny mean that people in the village know one another intimately and feel the sympathy that understanding brings in its train for even their most unpleasant neighbors. When Belinda comes to realize that Agatha Hoccleve regrets marrying her husband and is interested in another man, she develops some real fellow-feeling for this arrogant, pretentious woman. There is a sense in which no one in the village is alone or would fail to receive help if it were needed.

This comforting sense of the almost complete knowledge that prolonged association creates never again reaches the height it attained in *Some Tame Gazelle* and in the other early novels characters begin to make remarks about "M for Miscellaneous," the unknown factor that prevents one person from ever fully knowing another, remarks that are finally more typical of Pym's views concerning human relationships. But in the early novels following *Some Tame Gazelle*, communities, whether they are sections of London or other villages, remain quite intimate and small in scale. "So many parts of London have a peculiarly village or parochial atmosphere, that perhaps it is only a question of

choosing one's parish and fitting into it" (EW, 11), Mildred
Lathbury remarks. This is true not only of her own shabby
part of London, where the vicar is aware of every arrival in
the district and asks parishioners to "say a word" (16) encourag-
ing church attendance to newcomers, but also of the neighborhoods in which *A Glass of Blessings* and *An Unsuitable Attachment*
are set. The village that is *Jane and Prudence*'s main locale is
almost as close-knit as the village in *Some Tame Gazelle,* so that
Jane's charlady can literally tell her what each of her new neighbors will be eating for dinner on any given evening.

By the time Pym wrote *The Sweet Dove Died* in the mid-sixties,
all this had changed. Leonora Eyre is careful not to get to know
Miss Foxe, the woman who rents an upper flat in the house
Leonora has just purchased, so that she will *not* develop the
sort of sympathy for Miss Foxe that might limit her own freedom
of action in deciding what to do with the flat. "One has to be
tough with old people," Leonora tells a friend, "it's the only
way—otherwise they *encroach*" (50). Because this sort of ruthless
individualism based on cultivated ignorance has largely replaced
the old sense of responsibility based on intimate knowledge,
the London of *The Sweet Dove Died* is a frightening place, lacking
neighborhoods, where people hide their pain behind the "dis-
creetly glistening cream or white facades" (16) of their dwell-
ings.

Owing to the more attractive nature of its characters, *Quartet
in Autumn,* Pym's next novel, does not paint the same portrait
of London as a place of ruthless coldness that we get in *The
Sweet Dove Died,* but neither is it the cozy parochial London
of the early novels. The four coworkers of *Quartet in Autumn*
see a good deal of one another, but only during the leisure
moments of the working day, for they fear and avoid social
intimacies. Making even the simplest social gesture proves too
much for them. On Letty and Marcia's retirement, Edwin thinks
that "perhaps they should have given the women a present of
some kind—but *what?* He and Norman had discussed it, but
decided in the end that it was altogether too difficult. 'They
wouldn't expect it—it would only embarrass them,' they had
concluded" (107). The thought of meeting their coworkers outside the office brings on a paroxysm of social tension: "But
what are we going to talk about, once we've asked them how

they are and all that?'' (127). So, although the coworkers are
indeed one another's most intimate human contacts, they aren't
as intimate as they might be, and know about one another only
what can be learned from public conduct.

In the course of the novel, Marcia goes "round the bend"
into complete insanity without the other three more than dimly
registering the thought that she is becoming a bit odder than
she once was. This could not have happened to anyone in *Some
Tame Gazelle*. Nonetheless, people do care about their fellow
men in *Quartet in Autumn;* it's just that the fragmentation and
the fear characterizing modern big city life as Pym sees it here
prevent their concern from finding effective means of expression. The close contact necessary for real understanding and
effectual help is absent. When Edwin finally nerves himself to
overcome his fear of contact and visit Marcia, he is too late,
and finds her in a state of collapse from which she does not
recover. All he can do is arrange her funeral, and he is only
marginally more successful in the attempts he makes, toward
the close of the novel, to alleviate Letty's loneliness.

In *A Few Green Leaves* Pym returns to the village setting she
had used in some of her early novels and portrays a community
that, though tiny, has not escaped the fragmentation characterizing the London world of the other late books. Many people
living in the village can remember the days when the squire
resided in the manor house and when members of the lower
classes lived in the village proper, in close contact with the
gentry. But now the manor has an absentee owner, while "most
of the original inhabitants" live in the new housing estate "on
the outskirts of the village and one [doesn't] have much contact
with them" (40). Intimate associations crossing class lines have
disappeared and one elderly inhabitant remarks mournfully that
"we haven't got any kind of centre to the village now" (116).
In this fragmented village indifference, ignorance, and hostility
are realities that cannot be overlooked.

But as the foregoing remarks may have suggested, the problem is not entirely one of scale. The village of *A Few Green
Leaves* is not, as far as one can tell, much bigger than the earlier
villages, nor is the disappearance of small parochial neighborhoods within London to be attributed to an increase in the
total size of the metropolis. One reason for the loss of communal

intimacy that the later novels chart is the disappearance of the church as the central social institution and its replacement in that role by the "helping professions" of medicine and social work. In the villages of *Some Tame Gazelle* and *Jane and Prudence,* the church is the center for the provision of guidance and charity; people don't cease to attend because Henry Hoccleve is a very inadequate clergyman, whose incomprehensible sermons are filled with obscure quotations. In London, it is the church that creates a neighborhood and gives it a villagelike character.

Church services in Pym's early novels are nearly always well attended, sometimes uncomfortably so. "The service began and was both beautiful and exhausting because there were so many people," says Wilmet Forsyth, in *A Glass of Blessings,* of a midnight mass she goes to, "and it was after half past one before we had finished. Getting out of church was slow and there was a crowd of people in the porch exchanging greetings with the clergy and with each other. I noticed Mr. Coleman . . . with two of the servers—the thurifer, who worked in a garage, and another who taught in a secondary modern school" (AGB, 100). At a parish gathering later in the novel, Wilmet returns to this idea that the church unites people of differing classes and backgrounds, thinking that "it seemed as if the church should be the place where all worlds could meet, and looking around me I saw that in a sense this was so. If people remained outside, it was our—even *my*—duty to try to bring them in" (209).

The last three novels, however, though they assert the continued relevance of Christianity to the lives of intelligent people, in one way or another portray the decline of the church as a social institution. *The Sweet Dove Died* does not contain a single character who has any real interest in religion. *Quartet in Autumn* does portray some churchgoing characters, but their Christianity is in various ways less satisfactory than the faith of many characters in the early novels. For Edwin the ceremonies and traditions of the church are far more important than either piety or morality. Charitable only in a minimal way, Edwin "goes around to a lot of churches, as it takes his fancy" (143), sampling the different varieties of service, and he meditates with real authority and enthusiasm not on the church's teaching, but rather on "the soothing rhythm of the church's year. All Saints' today,

then All Souls'. . . . Then would come Advent followed
closely—too closely, it often seemed—by Christmas. After
Christmas came Boxing Day, the Feast of St. Stephen. . . ."
(73), and so on. For Letty, Christianity is "a grey, formal, respectable thing of measured observances and mild general undemanding kindness to all" (66). In *A Few Green Leaves,* the village
clergyman Tom Dagnall is perhaps the most ideal Christian in
any of Pym's novels, but he is also one of only a few Christians.
The young people in this novel, ominously, have no use for
the church.

   And not only are there few Christian characters in Pym's
last novels, but church attendance in general has fallen off dramatically. Through the eyes of the elderly Edwin, in *Quartet
in Autumn,* we see the degree to which the church has lost
popularity and influence, a topic that didn't come up in *The
Sweet Dove Died* because none of its characters was sufficiently
interested in religion to notice this decline. When Edwin's friend
Father Gellibrand suggests altering the service at his church
so that each person turns to the one next to him with "a kiss
of peace," Edwin, "remembering the emptiness of the church
at the service they had just attended . . . was . . . doubtful—
not more than half a dozen dotted among the echoing pews
and nobody standing next to anybody to make any kind of
gesture. . . . He often thought regretfully of those days of the
Anglo-Catholic revival in the last century and even the more
sympathetic climate of twenty years ago" (15). Again and again
Edwin notes a London church closed as "redundant," or a reduc-
tion in the number and variety of the services available, and
some of the parishes involved are the very ones that appeared
in a flourishing state in Pym's earlier novels. In *A Few Green
Leaves,* Tom's church is so empty that he must resort to exercises
of imagination to fill it: "One morning Tom went into the
church, as he so often did, to spend half an hour or so, not
exactly to meditate or pray but to wander in a random fashion
round the aisles, letting his thoughts dwell on various people
in the village. This was in its way a kind of prayer, like bringing
them into the church which so few of them actually visited,
or never darkened its doors, as a more dramatic phrase has
it" (62).

   Both *Quartet in Autumn* and *A Few Green Leaves* make it clear that the influence that the church is losing has passed into the hands of the scientific professions. Marcia Ivory, terminally ill, retired, and batty, becomes the responsibility of the social services. But neither the National Health doctors who treat Marcia's cancer, nor the social worker who visits her, knows Marcia in the intimate way that her parish priest or village neighbors might have done at an earlier time and so none of these "experts," each fixated on the one particular aspect of Marcia in which he or she *is* expert, notices how desperate her overall condition really is. Marcia's general practitioner is disturbed by her appearance and even makes a "glib, but accurate diagnosis" of her mental state: "Odd, difficult" (QA, 152). After "wondering what on earth to do with her," he decides to pass the buck: "No doubt Strong's boys would suggest something" (153). At Mr. Strong's clinic, however, she sees a doctor who is far less able than the general practitioner to understand what terrible shape she is in. This "golden-haired boy, a houseman doing his training in surgery . . . hardly knew what to expect of a woman in her sixties," and after asking himself vaguely, "were they always as thin as this?" (49), sends her home without realizing that she is starving herself to death. In the well-intentioned, but hopelessly fragmented and overgrown world of London social services, Marcia is everyone's responsibility and hence no one's responsibility. Medical and sociological euphemisms fail to explain adequately the events preceding Marcia's death—she had "definitely been in a terminal situation," "there might possibly have been a lack of liaison" (187) among the agencies responsible for her welfare.

In *A Few Green Leaves* the village people prefer to go to the two local doctors for the advice and guidance they would once have sought from the rector, because "you might *talk* to the rector . . . but he couldn't give you a prescription. There was nothing in churchgoing equal to that triumphant moment when you came out of the surgery clutching the ritual scrap of paper" (13). And it is largely because the sciences and social sciences claim to be able to "give you a prescription," that is, provide reliable knowledge and guidance, while religion, at most, provides a framework within which you can think about your problems, that the latter is losing its influence.

When Dr. Martin Shrubsole tells his mother-in-law, Magdalen

Raven, that she will find her new bifocals "much better" than
the two pairs of glasses between which she had been alternating,
the old woman thinks with annoyance, "of course it was much
better—everything about her son-in-law was 'better,' Magdalen
Raven knew this perfectly well—good, better, best" (AFGL,
54). Living with Martin, Magdalen has become more aware
of the drawbacks of his facile and dictatorial assurance than
are his patients in general. *She* gravitates toward the diffident
Tom, but most of the villagers want Martin's certainty and optimism, delusive though they are.

In *Quartet in Autumn,* Edwin reflects on the nature of Ash
Wednesday, "evening Mass and the Imposition of Ashes, the
black smudge on the forehead, 'dust thou art and to dust shalt
thou return'—some people didn't like that, thought it 'morbid'
or 'not very nice' " (74). Mrs. Alexander's hymn to the effect
that "Within the churchyard, side by side / Are many long
low graves" is "not one they ever sang now; 'morbid' " (AFGL,
142), Tom Dagnall thinks. Because the church offers sobering
reflections on human mortality and imperfection, where science
offers "good, better, best," the latter is winning the battle for
control of men's minds, convincing people that the religious
point of view is unhealthily pessimistic. Yet for Pym, with her
belief that no pattern is ever certain or complete, that imperfect
understanding and imperfect communion *are* our lot on earth,
however many pleasures we may enjoy, this is an unfortunate
development. The sciences provide few answers in her books
and Martin Shrubsole is at his best when he uses common sense.
"If you *would* take hedgehogs into your house you'd get fleas"
(AFGL, 14), he thinks when an elderly village eccentric tells
him that itching flea bites are keeping her awake at night, and
it's about the most acceptable thought he has in the course of
the entire novel.

If science is replacing religion in the world of Pym's late
novels, it is equally true and unfortunate that the social sciences
and the mass media are also replacing literature as tools for
comprehending the world. Literature, like religion, is what one
makes of it, and unpleasant people like Henry Hoccleve in
Some Tame Gazelle and Leonora Eyre and Ned in *The Sweet Dove
Died* may be highly literary without absorbing from the great
works they read and quote much that proves beneficial to their

conduct. But, as with religion once again, the right sort of person can obviously gain increased human awareness from literature, and many of Pym's characters, especially in her early books, do. When Tom Mallow tells Catherine Oliphant that he is "losing his faith" in anthropology, she wonders "what Victorian wives and mothers had done with their menfolk who had lost their faith. What had they said to them? Matthew Arnold, she thought idly, the last lines of Dover Beach coming into her mind. 'Ah, love, let us be true to one another,' she said softly" (LTA, 106). Too bad for Tom, who in his need for reassurance is turning away from the critical Catherine toward a more admiring young girl, that he can't see the relevance of the line to himself and says only, "I don't think your Victorian poets are much help these days" (LTA, 106). Tom may be losing his "faith" in social science, but he remains contemptuous of literature, which Catherine finds so helpful.

Literature, important to many characters in the early novels, is being gradually replaced by television—which makes its unpleasant debut in *Less Than Angels,* and has become so important by the time of *A Few Green Leaves* that the narrator can simply assume that the main effect of an evening power failure will be to disrupt the "television viewing of most people in the village" (225)—as well as by popularized social science. *Quartet in Autumn* portrays a world that has largely jettisoned its literary traditions. The novel's first scene shows its four protagonists visiting a library on their lunch hours, each one, ironically, looking for something other than imaginative literature. Edwin goes to consult *Crockford's Clerical Dictionary,* Norman because he finds the library "a good place to sit" (2), and Marcia "to collect leaflets and pamphlets setting out various services available for the elderly" (2). Only Letty goes for books, but she never read much good fiction and has now given up even popular fiction as irrelevant to her own situation, and has turned to biography.

The number of times the characters in this novel quote even "the odd tag" (20) of poetry could be counted on the fingers of one hand. Feeling that she ought to do some serious reading after her retirement, Letty turns not to authors like "Jane Austen and Tolstoy" (3), who might have helped, or at least pleased her, but to the works of sociology, which are now held in higher esteem. Clearly Letty is wrong to blame herself for being "frozen with boredom, baffled and bogged down by incomprehensible jargon, continually looking at her watch" (117), as she tries to read these tomes. But, sure that they are valuable works, she concludes that "her brain had become atrophied. Had she indeed ever had a brain?" (117). The media and the social sciences are not more adequate substitutes for literature than they are for religion, and their success has impoverished Pym's world. As early as 1948 Pym had written prophetically in one of her diaries: "Television—the curiously shaped aerial on top of the house. A contrast with the church which has a cross."[3]

Like religion and literature, love plays a diminished role in Pym's last three novels. As we noted earlier in this chapter, Pym displays her characteristic tolerance in her attitudes toward love, understanding that it takes different forms in different lives. In her early novels, however, love usually does take a fairly satisfactory form. Siblings who live together, like Belinda and Harriet Bede or Julian and Winifred Malory in *Excellent Women,* are affectionate and close. Marriages, though not ecstatic, tend to be basically sound. Nicholas Cleveland is tolerant of Jane's eccentricities—"his poor Jane, he must let her go where she wanted" (JP, 116)—while Jane is never so bored with marriage as to forget that "a husband was someone to tell one's silly jokes to, to carry suitcases and do the tipping at hotels. . . . And . . . a great deal more than that" (10–11). Even the narcissistic characters, like Prudence Bates, are almost likable in their self-absorbtion; Prudence does not hurt her lovers, whose emotional response to her is minimal, and her comically superficial affairs provide her with what she regards as a rich life. The characters whose love chooses odd objects—Harriet Bede's curates or Edwin Pettigrew's animals—are usually happy with their choices.

In the last three novels, however, lovelessness, destructive narcissism, and the betrayal of love become more important. Only in the late novels do we find siblings, like Tom and Daphne Dagnall, living together in what verges on open dislike. Marriages are even fewer in these novels than in the earlier books, and they are far less satisfactory. Returning home, the widowed Edwin remembers his late wife and "could almost hear her voice, a little querulous, asking 'Is that you, Edwin?' As if it could be anyone else! Now he had all the freedom that loneliness brings—he could go to church as often as he liked, attend meetings that went on all evening, store stuff for jumble sales in the back room. . . . Edwin went upstairs to bed humming a favorite Office Hymn 'O Blest Creator of the Light' " (QA, 16). This is a rather grim thumbnail sketch of a marriage. Beatrix Howick in *A Few Green Leaves* got married in 1939 because "it was the sort of thing people were doing at that time and Beatrix had always felt that a woman should marry or at least have some kind of relationship with a man" (99–100). When her husband is killed at Dunkirk, Beatrix heaves a sigh of relief and turns her attention to other matters.

The narcissistic characters in the late novels, like Leonora Eyre and Ned in *The Sweet Dove Died,* are more destructively narcissistic than the vainest characters in the early books, really hurting, and sometimes liking to hurt, those who love them. And the characters in the last novels who have chosen an unusual, nonsexual object for their love—as Meg in *The Sweet Dove Died* loves Colin, a substitute for the child she "had always longed for" (31), and Liz in the same novel loves her Siamese cats—tend to find that object less satisfactory than did similar characters in the earlier books. For Liz, as for Meg, the object of her love is merely an unsatisfactory substitute for what she *really* wants: her ex-husband, who treated her cruelly. In *The Sweet Dove Died* the idea that people often betray love becomes much more important than it was in earlier novels. Colin deserts and wounds Meg repeatedly; Leonora's young friend James does the same to her. Though *The Sweet Dove Died* suggests that people have to go on loving, it also implies that love is necessarily so imperfect and unstable that there's a strong temptation to give up on it altogether, a darker view of love's possibilities than the early novels took.

It would be easy to exaggerate the differences between Pym's early and late novels. *The Sweet Dove Died* is something of an oddity among Pym's works, an attempt, in part, to strike a more modern note after *An Unsuitable Attachment* failed to please her publishers, but the worlds of *Quartet in Autumn* and *A Few Green Leaves* are, as their titles suggest, not truly wastelands without harmony, beauty, or love. In the latter novel, whose tone recovers some of the ebullience of Pym's early work, especially, there are characters like Tom for whom religion and literature are still alive, and characters like Emma Howick who are converted from the modern agnosticism and faith in social science they originally espoused. Nonetheless, it is true that most of the basically likable characters in Pym's last three novels lack the religious and literary backgrounds that might help them intelligently to direct and control their impulses.

For many of the decent characters in Pym's early novels a commitment to Christianity, or the knowledge of morals and the vicarious human experience that great literature can provide, controls and redeems their mild eccentricities. The road away from egotism is a clear and alluring one, marked by the signposts that Christian churches and English literature have been erecting for hundreds of years. In Pym's late novels, this road is so overgrown that it has become little more than a path, hard to locate and frequently ignored. And the sciences don't really offer an alternate route. Pym's pessimism in her last three novels (and to a degree in *An Unsuitable Attachment,* where many of the developments we have been charting here can be seen in their early stages) cannot be dismissed as the crotchetiness of an aging woman who believes with Doctor Johnson that "all change is of itself an evil" (STG, 251), or as the irritation of a good writer with a world that failed to appreciate her talent. The changes in English society that Pym sees with her usual clarity are changes that, by temperament and conviction, she was bound to deplore.

Chapter Four

The Early Novels
Some Tame Gazelle

Some Tame Gazelle is a bit like a Jane Austen novel stood on its head. The plot situation that Austen uses in every one of her novels except *Northanger Abbey* is this: a group of young, unmarried women, some of them sisters, are living peacefully in the country, when their peace is disturbed by the entrance of disruptive individuals into the previously quiet life of their village. The young women and their families must, through a process of difficult, yet ultimately beneficial change, adjust to the novelties of thought, feeling, manners, and morals that the disruptive characters have introduced. Whether these characters and the ideas they represent are absorbed, expelled, or changed, the process of dealing with them alters the world of the novel and helps the young characters to make their most significant decision—the choice of a marriage partner—properly. Hence the novels always end comically, with celebratory marriages that prove that significant lessons have indeed been learned.

In *Some Tame Gazelle,* too, a group of unmarried women, including a pair of sisters, Belinda and Harriet Bede, are living quietly in a country village. But here the single women are middle-aged rather than young, and when the disturber characters, Mr. Mold, a hard-drinking librarian, and Theodore Grote, bishop of the African diocese of Mbawawa, arrive, they too are getting on in years. As in Jane Austen, so here, the marriage choice is the pivot on which the plot, such as it is, turns. Harriet Bede already has a devoted suitor, Count Ricardo Bianco, who has been proposing to her at regular intervals for many years, and she speedily receives an offer from Mr. Mold as well. Harriet rejects Mr. Mold, reflecting that his "house might be semi-detached, and not at all in an advantageous position . . . it might be unkind to hurt his feelings . . . but a smart and floridly

handsome admirer in the Prime of Life would be much more
acceptable to her than a husband of the same description" (136).
But in rejecting Mr. Mold, Harriet does not turn, as the reader
might expect her to do, to the loving and loyal Count Bianco.
Instead, she decides that she would be mad to "change a comfortable life of spinsterhood in a country parish . . . for the unknown trials of matrimony" (136), and reaffirms her singleness
for good and all.

Belinda, in her turn, receives a proposal from Bishop Grote
which is nearly as funny as Mr. Collins's proposal to Elizabeth
Bennet. "Miss Bede, I am sure you must have realized—have
noticed, that is—my preference for you above all the other
ladies of the village . . . one hardly looks for beauty at our
time of life. . . . *She is not fair to outward view . . .* how does
Wordsworth put it? . . . Perhaps you are not accustomed to
receiving such offers? . . . Or perhaps it is some time since
you last had one? . . . We need not speak of love—one would
hardly expect that now" (222–24). Belinda not surprisingly refuses this unflattering offer, and Bishop Grote goes his way
undismayed, commenting, "Do not give it another thought,
Miss Bede. . . . I assure you that *I* shall not. After all we must
remember that *God moves in a mysterious way / His wonders to
perform"* (225). For neither Harriet nor Belinda do the disturber
characters bring either change or marriage. Instead, they enable
Belinda to realize just how contented she is with the life she
has been living and the moral standards by which she has been
living it. So the plot structure of the novel, with its rejection
of both marriage and change, represents an ironic reversal of
the comic form so clearly embodied in Jane Austen's works.
And as we shall see shortly, the fact that some of the minor
characters in *Some Tame Gazelle* do marry serves only to empha-
size this point.

What, then, is the nature of the single life to which both
Belinda and Harriet decide finally to cling? The first thing to
be noted is that it is not the loveless life, quite the contrary.
Belinda and Harriet love each other deeply. When Harriet tells
her sister that she has refused Mr. Mold, the "look of relief
that brightened Belinda's face was pathetic in its intensity. . . .
Belinda was so overcome with joy and relief at Harriet's news
that she kissed her impulsively and suggested that they should

have some meringues for tea, as Harriet was so fond of them"
(142).

But the two sisters have their own variations of romantic
love as well. For over thirty years, Belinda has been in love
with Archdeacon Henry Hoccleve, who in their student days
rejected her in favor of his ambitious and competitive wife,
Agatha, and who now through an accident of fate lives in a
vicarage that is virtually next door to Belinda and Harriet's
house. Harriet simply cherishes—with a mixture of motherly
and flirtatious concern, the sort of paradoxical emotion that Pym
is so good at describing—the local curate, whoever he may
be. So long as the curate is pale, young, and in need of cherishing, Harriet's feelings are intensely engaged. When a curate
marries or goes to labor among the London poor, Harriet simply
transfers her attentions to his successor. At the end of *Some
Tame Gazelle* a new curate arrives in the parish and as Harriet
points him out to Belinda "her face radiated joy and happiness"
(250). No sex here, but plenty of strong emotion, nonetheless.

The epigraph of *Some Tame Gazelle,* which Belinda quotes
to herself, comes from a poem by Thomas Haynes Bayly: "Some
tame gazelle, or some gentle dove, / Something to love, oh,
something to love." To have something, indeed anything, that
can be loved wholeheartedly is an absolute psychological impera-
tive for many of this novel's characters, and the novel soon
suggests that unrequited, or at least unfulfilled, love tends to
bring more happiness than does successful love culminating in
marriage. Because of the irrational nature of desire and the
imperfection of all human creatures, some disappointment, and
often great disappointment, accompanies the fruition of a love
affair. And so the lives of the spinster sisters in *Some Tame Gazelle*
are, ironically, both more contented and more romantic than
the lives of their married friends.

Both Belinda and his future wife, Agatha, loved Henry Hoccleve in their youth, but only Belinda still loves him thirty years
later. Handsome and capable of exerting great, if superficial,
charm on selected occasions, he is also an extremely difficult
man to live with, as Agatha has discovered. When Belinda goes
to the Hoccleves' to make arrangements for a church garden
party, she sees Henry "leaning out of one of the upper windows,
calling to Agatha, and he sounded very peevish. . . . It seemed

that the moths had gotten into the archdeacon's grey suit and
why had Agatha been so grossly neglectful as to let this happen?"
(24–25). No wonder that, of the two women on the lawn listening to this tirade, only Belinda, who didn't marry Henry, and
not Agatha, who did, is still capable of noticing, with a romantic
flutter, that "he looked so handsome in his dark green dressing
gown with his hair all ruffled" (24). Belinda feels "happy and
peaceful" when she can pass an evening with Henry. "For here
she was sitting on the sofa with the person she had loved well
and faithfully for thirty years, and whom she still saw as the
beautiful young man he had been then, although he was now
married and an archdeacon" (145). *Not* having married Henry
has done this for Belinda; Agatha, married and forced to deal
with Henry's faults every day of her life, cannot congratulate
herself on such fidelity.

A similar point can be made about Harriet and the curates.
Belinda finds it "odd that Harriet should always have been so
fond of curates. They were so immature and always made the
same kind of conversation" (17). And Belinda certainly seems
to have a point here: the curates are dull. When Mr. Donne,
the curate whom Harriet is cherishing during most of *Some Tame
Gazelle,* comes to dinner at the Bedes', he is the only one of
the guests who makes "suitable conversation for the interval
between arriving and sitting down to eat. 'Do you know,' he
was saying eagerly, 'there was quite a *nip* in the air this evening?
I shouldn't be surprised if we had frost' " (117). Though the
ultraproper Belinda approves of this sort of vacuous chat for
a dinner party where the guests aren't intimate with each other,
Mr. Donne *never* rises above it. Harriet flirts with him and
coddles him: " 'Now you must have a pear,' she insisted. . . .
The curate helped himself to a pear and began to peel it. He
seemed to be getting rather sticky and there was some giggling
and interchange of large handkerchiefs between him and Harriet" (16). But because his stay in the village must necessarily
be temporary, Harriet cannot really get to know him, to realize
fully, as the more detached Belinda does, how dull he is. Nor
need she see him grow old. For Harriet curates are a renewable
resource and so her relationships with them have a passion, a
freshness, a timelessness that no marriage could supply. The
curate of the moment is perpetually a beautiful young man,

full of possibilities. What woman's face ever quite "radiated joy and happiness" (250) when gazing at her husband of thirty years—as Harriet's does when she meets Mr. Donne's successor?

When, at the conclusion of *Some Tame Gazelle*, Mr. Donne marries Olivia Berridge, a don ten years older than himself who "does research in Middle English. . . . Something to do with *The Owl and the Nightingale*" (58), this marriage provides a contrast with Harriet's perpetual passion for curates, just as Henry and Agatha's marriage throws Belinda's perpetual passion for Henry into relief. Nothing could be more sensible and pleasant—or more passionless—than the union between Mr. Donne and Olivia. Before anything serious develops between them, Mr. Donne tells his friends that he thinks of Olivia "as an older sister" (91). Asked if Olivia is beautiful, " 'Well not exactly *beautiful*,' he said looking embarrassed, 'but very nice and so kind' " (91). Listening to this, Belinda thinks shrewdly, "Ah, had she been more beauteous and less kind, She might have found me of another mind" (91). Olivia perseveres, however, knitting socks for Mr. Donne and eventually proposing to him. Mr. Donne just goes along. Olivia is a thoroughly nice woman and will make Mr. Donne a good wife, but there is no intense feeling between them. Their marriage, like many marriages, is a compromise with reality—a compromise that Belinda and Harriet need never make.

Harriet's indefatigable suitor, Ricardo Bianco, has also discovered the advantages of passionate celibacy. He has chosen for his great love a woman who is fond of him, but who, because of her obsession with curates, will clearly never marry him or anyone else. Since Ricardo is a melancholy person, a state of ever-frustrated longing suits him perfectly. When he despairs temporarily, Belinda tells him, " 'I know she is fond of you'. . . and said that some day everything would be just as Ricardo wished. 'Then I shall ask her again,' he declared, fired with fresh courage and looking as if he were about to quote Dante or Tacitus [his favorite writers] at any moment; probably the former, Belinda thought, for it seemed unlikely that there would be anything suitable in Tacitus" (214). Despite the comedy, the intensity of verbs like "declared" and "fired," and the tendency to break rapturously into quotation prove the strength of Ricardo's feeling for Harriet.

Further, Ricardo's loyalty and stability contrast with the behavior of another middle-aged suitor, the Bishop of Mbawawa. After Belinda's refusal, the Bishop immediately proposes to his second choice, Connie Aspinall, a dreary spinster of the sort, actually quite rare in Pym's work, who would marry nearly anyone. According to Connie, Bishop Grote, apparently without embarrassment, claimed that "as soon as he came here he felt he was destined to find happiness, and that when he saw me he knew *it was to be*" (239). This amusing union seems trivial indeed when its emotional bases are compared with Ricardo's love for Harriet, or Belinda's for Henry, though it will doubtless be quite satisfactory to Connie and her husband.

Paradoxically, then, it is by *not* marrying that one keeps passion alive in *Some Tame Gazelle.* And there is a corollary proposition whose truth Belinda also proves: that to do little and eschew the ambition to achieve is perhaps the best way of keeping one's moral sensibilities tremblingly acute. This is the other positive value in the life of quiet spinsterhood that Belinda discovers and affirms at the end of the novel. In the course of the story, Belinda congratulates herself on *not* having done many things: going to tea with Henry, knitting him a pullover, proposing to him in her youth, and accepting Bishop Grote's proposal in her middle age. Refraining from action is never a source of regret to her, in part because she comes to see that inactivity has been beneficial to her character.

The person who strives to realize his or her own aims is likely to have less time and desire to take the interests of other people scrupulously into account than will the person who is quiet and contented with little, as the contrast between Belinda and Agatha suggests. Intent on forwarding Henry's ecclesiastical career, Agatha must expend her resources where they are most likely to pay off. The result is general pretentiousness, plus an ugly sort of domestic parsimony. "Very poor meals there," Agatha's seamstress remarks, "Mrs. Hoccleve doesn't keep a good table. At least, I never see any proof of it. An old dried-up scrap of cheese or a bit of cottage pie, *no* sweet sometimes. I've heard the maids say so, too, you know how these things get about" (52). Belinda, on the other hand, wanting little for herself, has both the inclination and the leisure to take scrupulous thought for others. After a morning spent in ill-fated, but

sincere, attempts to be kind to the very seamstress whom the
Hoccleves feed on scraps, Belinda finally realizes that her efforts
have been appreciated. Her "eyes filled with tears and she experienced one of those sudden moments of joy that sometimes
come to us in the middle of an ordinary day" (52). And being
only human, Belinda is pleased to reflect that Agatha is "just
the tiniest bit mean" (53), while she herself is generous.

Since manners are the social expression of a moral code, it
is perhaps not surprising that the kindly, scrupulous, leisured
Belinda should be preoccupied with propriety to a truly comic
extent. Belinda is very easily embarrassed, especially by anything
with the remotest sexual or scatological overtones, as the novel's
opening sentences suggest: "The new curate seemed quite a
nice young man, but what a pity it was that his combinations
showed, tucked carelessly into his socks, when he sat down.
Belinda had noticed it when they had met him for the first
time at the vicarage last week and had felt quite embarrassed"
(7).

Most of the time, however, Belinda's comically acute concern
with propriety cannot simply be laughed off as a spinster's prud-
ishness. Though the violations of propriety about which Belinda
worries are often so tiny or so remote that the reader cannot
take them very seriously, her concern is generally based on a
laudable desire to spare embarrassment and consider others'
rights. In a duty-letter to Agatha, who is on vacation, Belinda
writes, " 'The archdeacon preached a very fine sermon. . . .
We were all very much impressed. You will be glad to hear
that he is looking well and has a good appetite.' Here Belinda
paused and laid down her pen. Was this last sentence perhaps
a little presumptuous? Ought an archdeacon to be looking well
and eating with a good appetite when his wife was away? And
ought Belinda to write as if she knew about his appetite? She
turned to the letter again and added 'as far as I know' to the
sentence about the appetite" (139–40). The decision Belinda
makes here isn't very momentous and the passage describing
it is funny, but underlying Belinda's struggle over this tiny issue
of propriety is a desire not to meddle between husband and
wife or to exaggerate her own intimacy with Henry. Agatha's
superficially elegant, but often unpleasantly condescending manners again form the contrast.

Like some other Pym characters, however, Belinda is a bit
paradoxical. A little snobbery goes along with her kindness and
scrupulousness. After eating a serving of beans into which she
has seen her hostess accidentally drop some cigarette ash, Belinda congratulates herself on the heroic politeness she has displayed, concluding that "perhaps there was something after all
in being a gentlewoman" (184). It's hard to evaluate Belinda's
mixture of sweetness and pride, conventionality and insight,
vagueness and practicality. But paradoxical as she is, Belinda
doesn't move toward greater consistency in the course of *Some
Tame Gazelle;* rather she comes to realize that she is already a
very happy woman. As is so often the case in Pym's novels,
Belinda's pleasures are the more intense for their rarity. After
having supper with Henry while Agatha is away, Belinda thinks,
"It had been such a lovely evening. Just one evening like that
every thirty years or so. It might not seem much to other people,
but it was really all one needed to be happy" (158).

Belinda comes to see, in addition, that the ineffectuality, timidity, and general lack of sparkle, which make her envious of
the competent and successful Agatha, aren't really such serious
defects. Whenever Agatha meets Belinda, she snubs her, but
when it becomes apparent that Agatha has fallen in love with
a chance acquaintance, Bishop Grote, whose only appeal would
seem to be that his blandly vacuous personality is so different
from Henry's prickly one, Belinda realizes just how shallow
Agatha's claims to success really are. Belinda has a startling
new vision of Agatha when Bishop Grote confides in her that
Agatha has knitted him some socks that " 'are not quite long
enough in the foot.' The Bishop laughed with a silly, bleating
noise. 'Quite between ourselves, of course,' he added. 'Of
course,' repeated Belinda, closing the front door behind him.
She felt that she could almost love Agatha as a sister now . . .
the pathos of the socks not quite long enough in the foot. To
think of Agatha as pathetic was something so new that Belinda
had to sit down on a chair in the hall, quite overcome by the
sensation" (226).

It is typical of Pym that the small detail of the ill-made socks
should have such significance in helping Belinda to see the pathetic nature of Agatha's pretentions. Meeting Agatha at Mr.
Donne's wedding, Belinda is actually pleased to see her old

adversary's defenses back in place, so painful has she found the spectacle of an Agatha uncertain, carried away by undignified emotions, and longing for what she cannot have. " 'I'm not really very used to drinking champagne,' Belinda admitted. 'Aren't you?' Agatha gave a little social laugh, which would normally have crushed Belinda. . . . But today she . . . was almost glad to be able to see Agatha as her old self again. . . . It was so much easier to bear the burden of one's own pathos than that of somebody else. Indeed, perhaps the very recognition of it in oneself meant that it didn't exist" (248).

This insight sets the stage for the wonderful conclusion of *Some Tame Gazelle* at the wedding of Mr. Donne and Olivia Berridge. It looks like the celebratory marriage that traditionally concludes comedy. Everyone is there and everyone is happy, including the unpleasant Agatha. What is really being celebrated here, however, is not marriage, but singleness, not worldly success, but rather the refusal to pursue it, not progress, but acceptance of things as they are. Mr. Donne and Olivia will get along pleasantly and Agatha has her position and her clothes from the best houses to console her for her unsatisfactory marriage, but it is the spinsters Belinda and Harriet who experience something close to ecstasy as they contemplate an unchanged future. Harriet points out the new curate to Belinda: "He was dark and rather Italian looking, paler and more hollow cheeked than the others. Now Belinda understood her sister's joy and suddenly she realized that she too was happier than she had been for a long time. For now everything would be as it had been before those two disturbing characters Mr. Mold and Bishop Grote appeared in the village. . . . Belinda . . . could only be grateful that their lives were to be so little changed" (251).

Excellent Women

More than any of Pym's other novels, *Excellent Women* is a one-character book, which depends for its interest largely on the appealing and complex personality of its narrator, Mildred Lathbury, an unmarried clergyman's daughter of thirty-one, who hastens to assure the reader that she is "not at all like Jane Eyre, who must have given hope to so many plain women who

tell their stories in the first person" (7). Mildred's subtle consciousness not only provides the center of the story, but virtually
is the story itself, and theme, in the sense of organizing idea,
is downplayed to a rather surprising degree.

When *Excellent Women* opens, Mildred has been living for
several years in a run-down London neighborhood, supported
by a small private income and a part-time clerical job at a society
for the aid of distressed gentlewomen. She has quickly become
a pillar of a local Anglican church and often marvels that "I
should have managed to make a life for myself in London so
very much like the life I had lived in a country rectory" (11),
before her parents died. The only rebellion against the habits
and values of her upbringing in which Mildred has indulged
concerns her choice of a church. St. Mary's, whose unworldly
vicar, Julian Malory, and his even more unworldly sister Winifred Malory have become her closest friends, is an Anglo-Catholic church of which Mildred's parents "would not have approved
at all. . . . I could imagine my mother, her lips pursed, shaking
her head and breathing in a frightened whisper, 'Incense'"
(11). As Mildred herself remarks, this is indeed, a "harmless
way" (11) to rebel against one's upbringing.

Superficially Mildred conforms to the popular stereotype of
an excellent woman: the spinster engaged in good works. She
has "never been very much given to falling in love. . . . Of
course there had been a curate or two in my school days and
later a bank clerk who read the lessons, but none of these passions had gone very deep" (44). "Mousy and rather plain,"
Mildred draws "attention to these qualities with my shapeless
overall . . . old fawn skirt" (7) and other nondescript clothes.
And more than any other character in Pym's novels, Mildred
is engaged in a conscious and continuous effort to live according
to the teachings of Christianity. Feeling an impulse of dislike
toward a new acquaintance, Mildred begins to "reproach myself
for lack of Christian charity." Debating the issue internally she
wonders, "but must we always like everybody?" and answers
rather primly, "perhaps not, but we must not pass judgement
on them until we have known them a little longer than one
hour. In fact, it was not our business to judge at all" (10).
Mildred's constant habit of self-examination and the persistent
way she uses the vocabulary of moral evaluation—right, wrong,

guilt, shame, and so forth—distinguish her even from the most pious of Pym's other heroines, as surely as does her habit of keeping devotional books on her bedside table.

But there is another side to Mildred's personality, perhaps symbolized by the fact that the religious works must share her bed table with a collection of cookery books, which she finds at least equally consoling to read in moments of sleeplessness. On one such occasion she feels "rather glad" that her searching hand, which "might have chosen *Religio Medici* . . . had picked out *Chinese Cookery*" and she is soon "soothed into drowsiness" (20) by the earthly delights it describes. Mildred loves good food and she also has a rather sharp sense of humor, which, though she tries guiltily to repress it, occasionally takes her to the brink of unchristian malice. At a school reunion, Mildred observes that most of the participants take "a secret pleasure in belittling those of the Old Girls who had done well and rejoicing over those who had failed to fulfill their early promise" (109). Even as she plays her chosen role of excellent woman, Mildred watches herself with an ironic, critical eye: "Platitudes flowed easily from me," she notes as she makes suitable conversation on one sticky social occasion, "perhaps because, with my parochial experience, I know myself to be capable of dealing with most of the stock situations or even the great moments of life—birth, marriage, death, the successful jumble sale, the garden fete spoilt by bad weather" (6). Mildred cannot constantly achieve the Christian excellence she aims at, for the streak in her personality which she calls her "perverseness" (19) leads not only to impulses of irritation and malice, but also to an occasional rejection of the very virtues she usually seeks. Contemplating the sorts of people who might be desirable tenants for an unfurnished flat in the Malorys' vicarage—"Canon's widows, clergymen's sons, Anglo-Catholic gentlewomen (non-smokers), church people (regular communicants)"—Mildred thinks glumly that they are "all so worthy that they sounded almost unpleasant" (17). Mildred values worthiness, but is also quite aware of its association with dullness, in herself and others.

Until the Napiers move into her house, Mildred's experience with unworthy, but perhaps interesting, people has been very limited. During the war she worked for the Censorship Bureau, where she "learned much of the wickednesses of human nature," but since most of this knowledge "was at second hand" (46), she doesn't think she really understands worldliness any better than do her friends, the incredibly innocent Malorys. So the arrival of the Napiers—attractive, but not morally admirable—proves to be the catalyst that crystallizes Mildred's latent dissatisfaction with her life as an "excellent woman."

Helena Napier moves into the flat below Mildred's while her husband, Rocky, a naval officer, is still stationed in Italy, where his wartime job consisted of arranging an admiral's social life and being kind to awkward Wren officers at the admiral's cocktail parties. Rocky's charm was a byword throughout Italy, as Helena quickly lets Mildred know, but even before the charming Rocky's arrival, the disturbing contrast to the excellent women of Mildred's circle that Helena presents has begun to upset the delicate balance between the two sides of Mildred's personality. Pretty, vivacious, fashionably dressed, useless in the kitchen, and not a believer, Helena has a husband and a career as an anthropologist as well. When Mildred meets her, she has just returned from a field trip to Africa, bringing with her notes on matrilineal kin groups and a one-sided attachment to her collaborator, Everard Bone. Although Mildred finds Helena's liberated attitudes to be rather comically predictable—noting wryly, for example, that Helena "feel[s] bound" to announce that "of course she had no use for churchgoing" (7) at the earliest possible moment, and that she speaks "almost proudly" (8) of her own domestic incompetence—she is also intrigued by the possibilities Helena represents. So even before Rocky arrives, Helena has made Mildred feel "spinsterish and 'set' in [her] ways" and so self-conscious about her dowdy clothes that she considers buying a new dressing gown, "something long and warm in a rich color" (19) in case she should meet one of the Napiers at the door of the bathroom they all share.

When Rocky returns from Italy, Mildred's dissatisfaction with her quiet life becomes more intense. Where Helena evoked a mixed response of dislike, disapproval, amusement, and envy, Mildred finds Rocky almost totally charming. Rocky is not only handsome and elegant, he is also—an attribute rare among the men in Pym's novels—amusing in an unfailingly courteous and appreciative way that makes even the dullest people feel entertaining. Mildred quickly sees that "it was part of his charm that he could make people like that feel at ease" (38), but this insight doesn't help her resist him.

On the evening she meets Rocky, Mildred significantly forgets to say her prayers. She takes "to using a little more make-up," her hair is "more carefully arranged," her clothes "a little less drab" (100). She becomes dissatisfied with her dreary underwear, loses faith in the consoling powers of tea, the harmless stimulant invariably served at church gatherings, and begins to experiment with alcohol, as Rocky, Helena, and Everard do. When Helena asks her if she doesn't think Rocky more attractive than Everard, Mildred is embarrassed, for she is "not used to discussing people in such terms," and makes an attempt to continue the discussion in the less sexually charged language she commonly employs: "Well, yes. I do think he is nicer" (96). However, Mildred has to admit to herself "that 'attractive' was a better word than 'nice' and expressed my feeling about Rocky more accurately" (96), though she continues to respect the proprieties by concealing that feeling. When Rocky, after a quarrel with Helena, moves out of the flat, Mildred goes to the window to watch his retreating taxi and then comments, "The effects of shock and grief are too well known to need description and I stood at the window for a long time. At last I did make a cup of tea, but I could not eat anything. There seemed to be a great weight inside me" (167). The woman who "would never do anything wrong or foolish" (44) has fallen in love with a married man.

As the Napiers, with the sexuality and hedonism that they so seductively embody, have disturbed Mildred's satisfaction in her "peaceful and happy" (120) life by moving in below her, so an equally potent disturbing force has entered the Malorys' vicarage in the person of Allegra Gray, a beautiful and youngish clergyman's widow who has rented their upper flat. Because Mildred is a far more observant and self-aware person than either of the Malorys, she comes to understand the nature of her attraction to Rocky much better than Julian ever does his infatuation with Mrs. Gray. Julian believes that his feelings for Mrs. Gray are as altruistic and moral in nature as his other motivations have always been. Discussing his engagement to Mrs. Gray with Mildred, Julian takes this line: "Allegra is a very sweet person and she has had a hard life . . . she is an

orphan" (133), he says solemnly, provoking Mildred to retort
sharply that "of course a lot of people over thirty are orphans"
(133). After he has quarrelled with Mrs. Gray, Julian tells Mildred sadly that he "thought her such a fine person" (211) when
he asked her to marry him.

Of course, Mrs. Gray's real attractions for Julian are very
similar to Rocky's for Mildred: she is pretty, "too nicely dressed
for a clergyman's widow" (57), clever with makeup, and capable
of being quite charming when she wishes. On occasion, her
wit, like Rocky's, is a bit naughty: "I always feel that one *ought*
to give men the opportunity for self-sacrifice; their natures are
so much less noble than ours" (83), she says maliciously as
she accepts a gift from Julian. Though she is transparently dishon-
est and manipulative in a way that Rocky, with his natural charm
and real kindness, is not, Mrs. Gray is clearly a parallel character,
and her effect on Julian, who advocated clerical celibacy and
lived for others before he met her, is identical to Rocky's effect
on Mildred.

In the end the disturber characters remove themselves from
both Julian's and Mildred's lives—Julian, who never really understands what has happened to him, returns to the life he lived
before he met Mrs. Gray, and Mildred, as befits her more complex personality, makes a more conscious decision about what
to do with the longings of which her relationship with Rocky
has made her aware. Should she return to being one of the
"observers of life," a person who says, as her old friend William
Caldicote advises her to do, "let other people get married"
(70), a spinster involved and interested primarily in "other people's business" (5)? Or should Mildred try to keep desire in
her own life?

By the time Rocky moves out of his flat, Mildred is clearly
aware of the problem and has decided that she must remain
what her nature and upbringing have made her. Excellent
women like herself, she tells Everard Bone, "are not for marrying. . . . They are for being unmarried . . . and by that I mean
a positive rather than a negative state." "Poor things, aren't
they allowed to have the normal feelings, then?" he asks, and
Mildred answers staunchly, "Oh, yes, but nothing can be done
about them" (190). It is not the excellent women who marry,
Mildred thinks, but "people like Allegra Gray, who was no

good at sewing, and Helena Napier, who left all the washing up" (170), women who know how to assert themselves and make their sexuality felt in a way that Mildred cannot emulate. "I can't change now. I'm afraid it's too late" (170), Mildred says, and the reader agrees. In spite of Rocky's disturbing effect on her, the excellent woman side of Mildred's personality remains in control.

One of the major ironies of the novel, however, is that Mildred is wrong when she says that excellent women are not for marrying, though quite right that they are not "for the other things" (189). A certain sort of man may well want an excellent woman for a wife, and with such a man she may enjoy an "excellent" marriage—stable, dull, and founded on *her* self-sacrifice in *his* interest—a very different sort of marriage from "the Napiers' rather unstable arrangement," (125) which is built upon the shifting sands of sexual magnetism and personal charm. By the close of *Excellent Women* it has become clear that Mildred is to make such a marriage with Everard Bone, whose extremely glamorous exterior gives no clue to his conservative, practical nature. Through her marriage with Everard, the only man in the novel who "could consider marrying an excellent woman" (189), Mildred avoids celibacy, but finds little sexuality or romance. Their union will be an extension of her habits of duty and self-sacrifice into a new field of endeavor.

It is one of the ironies of sex that the gay, irreverent Helena Napier should develop a "sudden irrational passion" (225) for the cautious Everard, when in fact she is much better suited to her husband Rocky. Helena is, however, passionately devoted to anthropology, a passion that Rocky definitely does not share and that Helena thinks she *can* share with Everard. But Helena is wrong, for Everard, though a serious anthropologist, is passionate about nothing, including anthropology. When Mildred asks him if field work is fun and congratulates him on the feeling of achievement his work must bring, Everard answers in a very characteristic tone: "Fun is hardly the word. . . . It's very hard work, learning an impossibly difficult language, then endless questionings and statistics, writing up notes and all the rest of it. . . . Achievement? . . . I sometimes wonder if it isn't all a waste of time" (35). What Everard is really looking for in a wife is someone who can help him with the least interesting

aspects of his work—proofreading and indexing—and he would
never allow his wife the liberty Helena has with Rocky. Though
Rocky may want Helena to help with the washing up—he enjoys
cooking, but like other Pym males he does only what he enjoys
and draws the line at any sort of cleaning—he certainly isn't
trying to turn her into a domestic servant. When Helena leaves
Rocky, Everard responds with his usual caution, fleeing to a
meeting of the Prehistoric Society, which he has joined only
because she is not a member, in order to escape any involvement
with her imprudence. "Hiding from a woman behind a cloak
of prehistory" (181), Mildred wryly remarks. Earlier, he actually
asked Mildred to be the bearer of a message to Helena, telling
her that he does not love her!

It is mainly because of Mildred's willingness to undertake
this sort of task that Everard becomes interested in her, as Mildred herself is well aware. And the relationship that develops
between Mildred and Everard is interesting precisely because
of Pym's refusal to romanticize it. Everard and Mildred are
sometimes able to talk pleasantly together, but Everard never
establishes the easy rapport with Mildred that Rocky effects
on their first meeting. A chat with Everard leaves Mildred "feeling like Alice in Wonderland" (35), because of Everard's complete refusal to adapt his conversation, as Rocky does, to the
needs of his interlocutor. Even after it begins to seem likely
that Mildred and Everard will marry, she is still having trouble
communicating with him and when they manage to share a
small joke, she thinks with relief, "not an inspiring conversation,
but it would do" (253).

Everard is not merely stiff, ungracious, cowardly, and inept
where personal relations are concerned, he also has a coolly
exploitative attitude toward women, which he takes little trouble
to conceal. When Everard tells Mildred that he plans to marry
"a suitable person . . . a sensible sort of person" (188–89)
someday, she thinks he intends "to look for somebody to marry
as if [he] were going to buy a saucepan or a casserole" (188)
and that is pretty much what he does. He is pleased to hear
that Mildred is well organized and keeps an oven cloth hanging
on a nail by the cooker. "Well, you're a sensible person" (189),
he tells her approvingly.

Although Everard makes several social overtures toward Mildred in the course of the novel, he makes them only when he wants something from her. Thus, Everard invites Mildred for a drink because he needs her services as a mediator between himself and Helena. He takes her to his mother's house for dinner so that she, and not he, will have to bear the brunt of conversation with the bizarre Mrs. Bone, who has an obsessive hatred of birds, Jesuits, and woodworms. "I eat as many birds as possible . . . at least we can eat our enemies," she tells Mildred as she carves the chicken (149). Everard's lunch invitation is predicated on his desire to question Mildred about the Napiers' marital problems; his first dinner invitation is the result of his having "some meat to cook" (218) and no one to cook it for him. When Everard finally entertains Mildred at a nice meal prepared by his charwoman, this magnificent gesture turns out to be the preliminary to his asking her to do the proofreading and the index for his forthcoming book—without pay, of course. Only when Mildred meets Everard accidentally does she get off scot-free.

Everard responds to Mildred's excellence—her obvious exploitability—rather than to her feminine charms. Where Rocky compliments Mildred on her "charming new hat . . . the brown brings out the colour of your eyes which look like a good dark sherry" (86), Everard never notices her appearance at all. When Everard waylays Mildred in the street to take her for a drink and Mildred apologizes for the fact that she is "hatless and stockingless in an old cotton dress" (139), he tells her perfunctorily and without even glancing at her that "You seem to be very nicely dressed" (146). When she goes to dinner at his flat, Mildred experiments with a new dress and hairstyle and en route meets two acquaintances who both comment unfavorably on the result. "Why it's Mildred," says one, "but I hardly recognised you. You have a rather more *triste* appearance than usual" (250). Reaching the flat she waits, with shaken confidence, for Everard's reaction, but he says nothing and she concludes "that he evidently did not think I looked any different from usual" (252). Indeed, he hasn't really bothered to look at all.

The only thing that suggests a mild sexual response to Mildred on Everard's part is his irritable reaction when she tells him that Julian Malory's engagement to Mrs. Gray has been broken

off. Since Mildred announces this news immediately after she
has refused to go to Everard's flat and cook his dinner, and
since Everard, in common with virtually everyone Mildred
knows, regards a romance between her and Julian as both suitable and likely, Everard's "stiff and unfriendly" (219) response
certainly implies jealousy. But the kind of jealousy that is being
suggested seems questionable. Everard may be even more annoyed at the thought that Mildred intends to cook Julian's dinner
instead of his own, than at the thought that Mildred might be
falling in love with Julian.

Mildred is under no illusions about Everard and when she
responds to his overtures she understands the sort of commitment she is making. When he calls to ask her to cook his dinner,
and she hears his voice on the telephone, she comments, "I
was instantly suspicious . . . what does he want? I wondered"
(218). After he makes his request Mildred sees herself "putting
a small joint into the oven and preparing vegetables. I could
feel my aching back bending over the sink" (218). But no
sooner has she refused to come and realized that her refusal
has offended Everard, than she begins "feeling uneasy and yet
not knowing why. I had not wanted to see Everard Bone and
the idea of having to cook his evening meal for him was more
than I could bear at the moment. And yet the thought of him
alone with his meat . . . was unbearable too" (219–20).

Essentially this is the choice Mildred must make: either she
must let Everard exploit her, or he will end their relationship,
leaving her to face both loneliness, and the guilt an excellent
woman feels if she refuses to be self-sacrificing and helpful.
No middle ground is really open to Mildred, and the comic
but real guilt she feels at the thought of Everard's cooking his
own meat—"He would puzzle over the heat of the oven, turning
it on and standing over it, watching the thermometer go up.
. . . I should have been nearly in tears at this point if I had
not pulled myself together" (220)—makes her choice for her.
The things Mildred has been planning to do that evening for
her own pleasure and benefit suddenly seem "uninteresting and
unnecessary," and since she cannot retract her refusal to Everard,
she confirms her commitment to service in general by deciding
"to go over to the vicarage to see if there was anything I could
do there" (220).

"Cooking his meat"—the phrase seems to have comic sexual overtones, as well as some sort of relevance to the customs of the primitive peoples Everard studies. Everard's sexual response to Mildred is fairly cool, but hers to him seems a bit warmer. Her fear that she may have ended their friendship by refusing to cook for him becomes first "a little nagging worry" (224)— a far cry from the strong emotions she felt over Rocky—and finally, as time passes, a "wish that I might cook his meat" (238). As she had done when suffering from an adolescent crush on a bank clerk who read the lessons in her father's church, so now Mildred finds herself walking where she is likely to encounter Everard. She feels jealousy at the thought that a professional acquaintance of Everard's may be the excellent woman whom Everard has selected to be his indexer, proofreader, cook, and wife. The association of Mildred's feeling for Everard with an earlier schoolgirl infatuation that she admits did not affect her very deeply, shows how much weaker that feeling is than was her powerful response to Rocky. A minimal, though perhaps adequate, degree of sexuality will be part of Mildred's marriage with Everard—nothing out of the ordinary, in spite of Everard's good looks.

Beyond this, little is going to change for Mildred, who will return to being, in Everard's service, the excellent woman that she was in the service of church, friends, and distressed gentlewomen, before the Napiers entered her life. "Before long I should be certain to find myself at his sink peeling potatoes and washing up; that would be a nice change when both proofreading and indexing began to pall. Was any man worth this burden? Probably not, but one shouldered it bravely and cheerfully and in the end it might turn out not to be so heavy after all" (255), she muses as she contemplates the future. What will the compensations be? In addition to lukewarm sexuality, Mildred may find quiet affection or at least respect, the satisfactions of being useful, and the joys of applying her talents for observation to a new milieu: "Perhaps I should be allowed to talk to Mrs. Bone about worms, birds, and Jesuits" (255), Mildred thinks hopefully. No longer a spinster, Mildred will nonetheless continue to be essentially an observer of and helper in the activities of others, as she predicted earlier when she said it was too late for her to change.

It therefore comes as no surprise to readers of Pym's later
novels to find that Everard and Mildred have indeed married,
to learn that Mildred is still doing his indexes, or to hear Everard,
arriving alone at a dinner party, begin to complain irritably
about how inconvenient it has been for *him* that *Mildred* is
suffering from flu. Pym resembles Anthony Trollope in choosing
to end several of her novels with marriages or approaches to
marriage, after having slyly undermined the value of marriage
in the body of the book. Where Jane Austen usually shows
the marriages of her minor characters to be unsatisfactory, but
then demonstrates that the heroine's marriage will be different
and better, neither Trollope nor Pym in *Excellent Women* chooses
to follow this pattern. In Trollope's work, marriage often means
slavery for a woman, and even at its best it is only a moderately
satisfactory accommodation of complex personalities to one another. *Excellent Women,* though more cheerful in tone than many
of Trollope's grim or grimly funny treatments of marriage,
doesn't essentially disagree. Mildred's marriage to Everard will
be based upon an excellent woman's habit of putting herself
second, while Helena and Rocky's arrangement will remain unstable and difficult. The ending of *Excellent Women* is as sly an
attack on the conventional conclusion of comedy with its celebratory marriages as is the ending of *Some Tame Gazelle.*

Jane and Prudence

Jane and Prudence is a novel about disillusionment and the
acceptance of one's own limitations. As the story opens two
old friends, Jane Cleveland, the forty-one-year-old wife of the
mild, kindly vicar, Nicholas, and Prudence Bates, a beautiful,
twenty-nine-year-old spinster whose unsatisfactory love affairs
have become her principal occupation, meet at an Oxford reunion of students and recall their lost youth. "Oh, those days
of wine and roses. They are *not* long" (7), says Jane, whose
disappointments are numerous. Once academically promising,
"she could hardly remember now what the subject of [her re-
search] was to have been;" perhaps "the influence of something
upon somebody" (11), as Virginia Woolf put it, perhaps a study
of her husband's namesake, the poet John Cleveland.
   Nor has Jane been much of a success as a clerical wife, though

when she was first engaged she "had taken great pleasure in imagining herself" in the role, "starting with Trollope and working through the Victorian novelists to the present day gallant, cheerful wives who ran large houses and families on far too little money" (8). But Jane is too fanciful, eccentric, and outspoken to succeed with her husband's conservative congregations. Her improprieties are small—a sympathetic remark about elderly atheists, "One feels that there is something of the ancient Greeks in them" (23), made to a clerical neighbor, or a comment about how well the seventeenth-century poets understood the importance of the body, voiced in the presence of a young girl—but in the circles Jane must frequent they create much uneasiness.

Jane also fails to fulfill her own ambitions either as a homemaker or as a mother. She has the large house, but cannot run it, for she is hopelessly undomestic, barely able to open a can, and totally incapable of giving her mind to practical details. She creates a "peculiar kind of desolation" (82) in the vicarages she inhabits. Further, though Jane's "picture of herself as a clergyman's wife had included a large Victorian family" (8), she has managed to produce only one child, Flora, an efficient young lady who is clearly in reaction against her mother's disorderliness and who has taken over many of her mother's housekeeping duties.

If Jane Cleveland, at the opening of the novel, is trying to deal with twenty years of failure, Prudence Bates is only just beginning to suspect that she may not succeed. From an early age the extraordinarily lovely Prudence was pursued by numerous suitors, and she enjoyed the experience so much that she is now unable to terminate it by accepting one of them. And so Prudence had "got into the way of preferring unsatisfactory love affairs to any others . . . it was becoming almost a bad habit" (9). Prudence herself is not fully conscious of any of this, but she is becoming dimly aware that all is not well in her life. Beauty, admiration, and love affairs, Prudence knows, are supposed to be the forerunners of marriage, not ends in themselves, yet Prudence, who is lovely and admired, remains single, while her contemporaries with the "unpainted faces, the wispy hair, the dowdy clothes" are mostly married—"that was the strange and disconcerting thing" (9). Prudence has an uncomfortable consciousness "of being still unmarried" (8) and a feeling that she will become ridiculous if she does not marry soon, though it is clear that if left to herself she would prefer continuing with her love affairs to marrying. But there is a problem that threatens to interfere both with the love affairs and with marriage: age. When Prudence begins "to recall some of her own past triumphs . . . and to compare them with her present state," she wonders, "had there perhaps been a slight falling off lately?" (159).

The falling off, indeed, has been more than slight, for when the novel opens Prudence's only romantic attachment for over a year has been an unrequited passion for her married employer, Dr. Arthur Grampian, who did no more to encourage it than to take her hand one evening at the office and murmur, "Ah, Prudence. . . ."—a flirtatious gesture of which he quickly thought better (37). As Flora Cleveland notes with the detachment of youth, "the supply of suitable men isn't inexhaustible when one reaches [Prudence's] age" (191).

Jane's failure and Prudence's fear are revealed at the Oxford students' reunion in a general atmosphere of female disillusionment. Though their tutor, Miss Birkenshaw, likes "her Old Students to be clearly labelled" as having achieved happiness through marriage or "with novels or social work or a brilliant career in the civil service" (10), in fact none of these talented women "has really fulfilled her early promise" (11), and Miss Birkenshaw's summaries of their sources of happiness—"Mollie [has] the Settlement and her dogs" (10), and so forth—are comically oversimplified and exaggeratedly optimistic, though not totally false. Even Miss Birkenshaw herself is a rather disappointed woman: her "great work on the seventeenth-century metaphysical poets was still unfinished, would perhaps never be finished" (11).

Early in the novel, however, both Jane and Prudence have the opportunity to make something of a fresh start—and indeed an examination of how well a fresh start is likely to work in early middle age gives the novel's plot its impetus. Jane and Nicholas move to a country parish where, Jane hopes, "people will be less narrow and complacent" (12) than in the suburbs, and therefore, presumably, more tolerant of her own oddities. Here she hopes to be more successful as a clerical wife, though she has no serious plans to reform her own behavior. In her new parish Jane meets the recently widowed Fabian Driver, a handsome man of just the right age and social position for Prudence. Indulging a matchmaking impulse, Jane brings the two together and a highly conventional romance of "good food, flowers, soft lights, holding hands, sparkling eyes, kisses. . . ." (111) and so on, quickly develops.

It looks promising, for Fabian is Prudence's male counterpart. Like her, he is beautiful and attractive to the opposite sex. And like her, he feels compelled to use this attraction, so that throughout his long marriage he was involved in a series of love affairs as numerous as Prudence's own. For both Fabian and Prudence, the desire for admiration is a ruling passion. As the very beautiful are apt to do, they take an aesthetic, rather than a moral, or even a practical, approach to life, living in houses furnished with lovely, but uncomfortable, Regency antiques, and allowing their desire for admiration to draw them into extramarital attachments. Their vanity carries them both to ridiculous extremes: Prudence painting her eyelids "startlingly and embarrassingly green" (84), and Fabian placing a photograph of himself, instead of a headstone, on his dead wife's grave. Neither can make a real religious commitment because neither can find a church that seems, socially and aesthetically, to be a suitable setting. Passing the local Methodist chapel, Fabian thinks that "of course one couldn't go there; none of the people one knew went to chapel. . . . Even if truth were to be found there" (54). Prudence reflects on religion in similar terms.

But in the end these two soul mates do not marry, for they are too much alike to get along peacefully and each wants slavish admiration from the other. Prudence plans to redecorate Fabian's house, choosing a new wallpaper for Fabian's late wife's room and Fabian feels his control over his own setting threatened by this. The ritual compliment Fabian always pays her—"You're looking very lovely tonight, darling" (158)—is too perfunctory to satisfy Prudence, and yet is greater homage to another person's beauty than Fabian ever really wants to render. Prudence's carefully cultured conversation and her elegant letters, studded with quotations from Donne and Coventry Patmore, do not arouse Fabian's admiration as she intends, but merely make him feel inadequate and inferior. The more intelligent Prudence is, in turn, wounded in *her* vanity when Fabian's conversational inadequacy is displayed in public—his dullness reflects badly on her. Jane is quite right when she observes that "a beautiful wife would have been too much for Fabian, for one handsome person is enough in a marriage, if there is to be any beauty at all" (193).

Though Prudence finds Fabian "both boring and irritating" (192), she decides to accept him if he proposes. Her motives are nothing stronger than a desire to be suitably married and a sense that he can provide an appropriate setting for her, and so she is by no means heartbroken when he decides to marry Jessie Morrow, his plain, mousy, and not very young neighbor. In part, Jessie attracts Fabian because aesthetically she is no competition for him, but she makes a positive appeal to his vanity as well. For though she sees through Fabian's shallowness, self-deceit, and egotism, and occasionally lets him know that she does, Jessie truly loves Fabian, loves him so much as to feel "that any little defect could only make him more dear to her" (168). And to love a man without forgetting his shortcomings is perhaps to pay his powers of attraction the greatest compliment of all.

Forty-eight hours after her rupture with Fabian, Prudence has with obvious elation embarked on a new romance, though admittedly it is a romance with an undistinguished man in whom she would not have been interested five years earlier. Shortly afterwards two more men are showing faint signs of interest and Prudence suddenly feels "overwhelmed by the richness of her life" (222). And so the novel ends—Prudence has not consciously realized that the failure of this particular attempt to marry has any implications for the future, but on some subconscious level she has indeed affirmed her particular brand of singleness and acknowledged that the emotional excitements of unsuccessful love affairs delight her more than any marriage ever could. And this is true even though, as time passes, the love affairs are bound to decline in both quality and quantity, while Prudence's spinsterhood will make her increasingly absurd to the world in general. Fabian, who has accepted Jessie in part to escape from Prudence, and must now content himself with her admiration alone, is less pleased with the outcome: "Life with Jessie suddenly seemed a frightening prospect. . . .

It was as if a net had closed around him" (199). He has found love but cannot really appreciate it. And so both Fabian and Prudence conclude more or less as they began, locked within the tiny emotional spaces enclosed by their vanity.

Prudence and Fabian are capable of creating beautiful orderly surroundings for themselves, but are not capable of feeling much for others. Jane's problem is just the opposite. Her twenty years of marriage to Nicholas have proved a failure in every other respect, but their love for one another has never died. And though she mourns its loss of intensity, she knows that this loss is typical of marriage in general. When Prudence, on a visit to the Clevelands, paints her eyelids green in preparation for a party, Jane observes "that Nicholas was gazing at Prudence with admiration, it was quite noticeable. So it really did work. Jane studied her own face in the looking glass above the sideboard and it looked to her just the same as when Nicholas used to gaze at it with admiration. Would he look at her with renewed interest if she had green eyelids?" (84). As the light tone here implies, Jane knows that there is nothing seriously amiss between Nicholas and herself. Her relations with his parishioners, however, have not been equally successful and she hopes that she will be more popular as a vicar's wife in the new country parish where people are "somehow noble through contact with the earth and nature" (137). And at first Jane, with the lively imagination that makes her a joy to the reader and a trial to her husband's parishioners, does find the novelty of her situation stimulating and exciting. "Here in this parish, all this richness" (21), she thinks, on hearing her charwoman's description of the local scene.

Soon, however, it becomes apparent that a change of place has not cured Jane's problems as a clerical wife and that people in the country are no less petty than those in the suburbs. There is trouble among the churchwardens over matters so trivial that Jane is unable even to understand what is at issue. "For a moment, I almost thought it was something to do with the men's lavatory in the church hall, the cistern or something," she tells Nicholas perplexedly, "but how could that be?" (65). When she makes a joking remark during a tense Parochial Church Council discussion concerning a design for the cover of the parish magazine, Jane's humor is not appreciated. Nicholas rebukes her, "My dear, I wish you had not said what you did" (137), and thinks glumly "that there was, after all, something to be said for the celibacy of the clergy" (137). Jane runs from the room shouting, "Oh, if I had known it would be like this," and takes refuge in the bathroom, where the sight of some soap animals that Nicholas bought for himself in a whimsical moment "reminded her of her love for him" (137). Jane realizes she has no choice but to go on—her love for Nicholas commits her to that—and decides to "concentrate on the things she *could* do," as a clerical wife, adding doubtfully, "whatever they might be" (138).

Jane's realization that a country parish has not been the answer to her difficulties and her resolution to try harder to cure those difficulties are rewarded with only very moderate success. Incorrigibly original, she continues to say the wrong thing on many occasions. But then the small successes she does have in her attempts to tone herself down are extremely cheering to her. In Nicholas's absence, Jane receives a surprise call from his predecessor, Canon Pritchard, and his wife, pompous people who say things like, "We drove over to the Clevelands in the motor and stayed to luncheon" (149). Since Jane has always felt that the dull, respectable Pritchards were far more popular in the parish than she and Nicholas are, she is pleased when her charwoman, showing an unexpected "treasure-like quality" (148), protects her from the Pritchards' criticisms by magically producing a clean guest towel and a meal suitable to the occasion. During the visit, Jane is "very careful with her own comments, remembering how her tongue and curiosity were apt to run away with her" (148) and for once manages to produce small talk of the required sort: "It has been a mild spring. . . . My husband likes air, of course" (147). When her visitors leave, Jane is "rather pleased to have managed so well" (151), though fortunately for the reader she never again achieves such a high standard of dullness. At the same time that Jane makes slight progress in controlling her tongue, evidence accumulates to suggest that there *are* some people in the parish who actually prefer the eccentric Clevelands to the proper Pritchards. The reader, ironically, realizes just as Jane begins trying to change, that her unpopularity was never quite as great as she believed.

Jane's domestic efficiency also improves marginally. Early in the novel, she visits London to buy Christmas cards and devotional books for confirmation presents, but ends up wandering about aimlessly, looking at jars of foie gras and the latest religious fiction. In a parallel scene at the end of the novel, however, Jane does manage to concentrate for ten minutes and to buy the cards and the "little holy books" (218) for confirmation candidates that she is seeking, though it seems momentarily as if her fanciful meditations on what it might mean to say you were "just looking around" (218), in a religious bookshop— "just looking around the Anglican Church from one extreme to the other, perhaps climbing higher and higher, peeping over the top to have a look at Rome on the other side, and then drawing quickly back" (218)—will prevent her from completing her task. Returning home, Jane shows Nicholas the books and he tells her "Splendid, dear" (221). So the story concludes for Jane and Nicholas, two "essentially good people" (138). Jane has made more progress than Prudence, but she has not changed much either. For both women, the resolution has been one of accepting their own lives, with their symmetrically contrasted limitations and defects: Prudence can never love anyone but herself and Jane's love will never be manifested in fully practical forms. Both will, as Jane remarks at the end of the novel, "go blundering along in that state of life unto which it [has pleased] God to call us" (212).

Prudence and Jane are the protagonists of the novel and it is therefore Prudence who, among the many vain characters it contains, receives the most intense scrutiny. Though it becomes clear that Fabian, Prudence's opposite number, is even more narcissistic than she, he is comparatively only a minor character. Perhaps in order to make certain that readers will not erroneously conclude from Prudence's central position in the story that vanity and its attendant vice, selfishness, are characteristically female failings, Pym threads through *Jane and Prudence* what is undoubtedly her most sustained comic commentary on male egotism. Some of this commentary comes from the narrator, and some of it comes from Jane herself, for Jane, like several other Pym heroines, is a keen observer of male posturing.

The point that women encourage men to place their own desires first is made repeatedly in *Jane and Prudence,* especially through the characters of Mrs. Mayhew and Mrs. Crampton, two widows once used to coddling their husbands, and now feeling the lack of a man to pamper, who run a teashop in Jane's village. "Of course, a man must have meat" (30), Mrs. Mayhew seriously informs a skeptical Jane within seconds after they are first introduced to one another. Later, in the teashop, Mrs. Crampton, unbidden, serves Nicholas a lunch of two eggs, while giving Jane only one, explaining, again quite seriously, that "a man needs eggs" (51). Nicholas accepts "the implication that his needs were more important than his wife's with a certain amount of complacency . . ." (51). Later, another village woman remarks without the least irony both that "a man needs a cooked breakfast" (90), and "that men need company more than women do" (113).

Women spoil men not merely by catering to these imaginary needs and by excusing their misconduct with tolerant platitudes like "We know what men are," but also by offering them an intense, focused love and loyalty that they do little to deserve, but which can console them in the interstices of their busier lives. "Oh, but it was splendid the things women were doing for men all the time," Jane thinks when she is first introduced to Prudence's current "love," the undistinguished-looking Arthur Grampian, "making them feel . . . that they were loved and admired and desired when they were worthy of none of these things—enabling them to preen themselves and puff out their plumage like birds" (75).

The social and economic power of men, the fact that their work is taken more seriously and rewarded more generously than that of women, also nourishes their vanity even when they are not in female company: "Men alone, eating in a rather grand club with noble portals—and women alone, eating in a small, rather grimy restaurant which did a lunch for three and sixpence, including coffee" (41). In fact, when "Arthur Grampian was shaking the red pepper onto his smoked salmon" in such a club, Prudence "was having to choose between the Shepherd's pie and the stuffed marrow" (41) in such a restaurant. And so in this novel, though it takes great beauty to produce a really vain *woman* like Prudence, vain men are extremely common and can be as plain as Arthur Grampian. Seeing tears in Prudence's eyes at the office (in fact they are tears for Fabian), Arthur, sure she is crying because he has treated her coldly, is "gratified" and concludes happily "that he still retained his old power over women" (197).

Jane and Prudence contains a gallery of smug or selfish male characters rising in intensity from Nicholas, who says " 'Tea not ready yet?' . . . in the way men do, not pausing to consider that some woman may at that very moment be pouring the water into the pot" (63), through Edward Lyall, the local MP with his "continual references" to the "burden" (88) he bears, and the conceited Arthur Grampian, to Fabian Driver, who glances at his handsome reflection in a mirror and thinks complacently, "No wonder one had had to hurt people" (176). These men are experts in getting women to do their dirty work. Wondering how he can amuse Edward Lyall at a tea party, since "country vicars are perhaps not used to entertaining Members of Parliament," Nicholas thinks, "the women would see to it" (171), and relaxes again in his deck chair, while Fabian (in the manner of Everard Bone in *Excellent Women*) convinces Jane that it is *her* responsibility to tell Prudence that he has become engaged to Jessie.

This comedy culminates at the tea party mentioned above, where the men complain at length about their difficult lives, though none of them has anything like a nine-to-five job: "Fabian and Edward seemed to be trying to outdo each other in weariness, and even Nicholas was making some attempt to compete, detailing the number of services he had to take on Sundays and the many houses he had to visit during the week" (172). Later, when Jessie spills a cup of tea on Prudence's elegant new dress, ruining it, the men are "a little annoyed at having attention diverted from their weariness" (173) and leave the party in something of a huff. Surely the comic exposure of male egotism cannot go much farther than Pym takes it in *Jane and Prudence,* and so she succeeds in writing a novel that centers on the personality of a vain woman, yet dissents from the stereotypical notion that *female* is the adjective that most naturally modifies *vanity,* the noun.

Less Than Angels

While working at the International African Institute in the late forties and early fifties, Pym began to see how much her

own approach to the writing of fiction had in common with
the anthropologist's approach to the study of primitive cultures.
In her novels Pym charts the social behavior of men and women
whose lives—like the lives of primitive peoples before the development of anthropology—are not generally seen as valuable
or worthy of intense scrutiny. And in dealing with her chosen
"culture" of the unmarried, the quiet, the unsuccessful, Pym
cultivates, as we noted in chapter 2, an attitude of tolerant recep-
tiveness that is not very different from the anthropologist's attempt to understand the utility or value of the strange and
shocking customs of primitive societies. "No expression of disgust . . . must show on the face of the investigator," (124)
says one of the characters in *Less Than Angels,* quoting from
an anthropologist's manual—and Pym, too, tries to approach
potentially upsetting topics such as aging, isolation, failure, and
death without disgust or shrinking. The detachment from the
objects of one's study that enables one to see them without
either the sentimentality that can come from excessive sympathy,
or the harshness that can come from overly narrow standards
of judgment, is as important to Pym as it is to the profession
of anthropology itself.

Pym was always aware, as chapter 3 of this book tries to
demonstrate, that there are highly significant differences between the scientific approach to understanding human beings
in society and literary and religious approaches to the same
issues, but it is only in her last two novels, *Quartet in Autumn*
and *A Few Green Leaves,* that Pym became concerned enough
about these differences to explore their implications in some
depth. In *Less Than Angels,* one of the most lighthearted of
her serene early novels, Pym is not particularly interested in
discussing the tensions between social science and literature,
or the deficiencies of the former. Rather, she is playing humorously with a set of ideas suggested by her realization that a
certain kind of novelist can and often does use methods of observation that are essentially anthropological. So in *Less Than Angels*
Pym asks herself two questions: What kinds of people observe
their own society in anything like an anthropological manner?
And, what would we discover if we applied anthropological
techniques of detached observation and analysis to the customs
and rituals of modern England, including even the rituals of
the anthropological profession itself?

Less Than Angels contains many characters who either are anthropologists or else resemble anthropologists in being detached observers of the social world around them. But their detachment is, in the latter case, of a different sort from that of the practicing anthropologist. Mabel Swan and Rhoda Wellcome, the mother and aunt of Dierdre Swan, a young student of anthropology, live together the comfortable lives of housebound suburban women. Lacking activities, they become observers of a peculiar kind. Where anthropologists observe customs as closely as possible while trying to keep their intellectual distance, Mabel and Rhoda take the opposite approach. Physically separated from the objects of their study—to wit, their neighbors—on whom they gaze from behind the curtains of their upstairs windows, Mabel and Rhoda completely lack intellectual distance and can evaluate the behavior they observe only in terms of one very parochial standard of judgment. Seeing that their new neighbor, Alaric Lydgate, a retired colonial official, is planning to beat his rugs in the garden at supper time, Rhoda is shocked at his violation of the only set of customs she knows—customs that, she assumes, have some sort of basis in reason—and comments, "The morning is really the time to do that. . . . If everybody were to beat their rugs in the evening, just think of the noise!" (33).

Catherine Oliphant, the mistress of a young anthropologist, Tom Mallow, and by profession a writer of romantic fiction and articles for women's magazines, is a more successful observer of the world around her than Rhoda and Mabel. Catherine knows that as a writer she must "draw her inspiration from daily life" (7), and is constantly on the lookout for the "odd details [that] often came in useful" (27). But Catherine is, in fact, more detached in her observation of social patterns than the most detached of practicing anthropologists. For she must stand back not only from everyday life, the subject of her study, but also from the stories and articles that are the product of her labor—because she knows that her writings ultimately distort the domestic reality in which they pretend to be grounded, in order to satisfy the desires and fantasies of her audience. So, ironically detached from her own work as a more serious writer would hardly be, Catherine becomes a sort of informal anthropologist of romantic fiction and its conventions: "She imagined women under the drier at the hairdresser's turning the pages lazily and coming to 'The Rose Garden' by Catherine Oliphant. They would read the first page, the one that had the drawing of a girl standing with a rose in her hand and a man, handsomer than any real man could possibly be, standing behind her with an anguished expression on his face . . ." (27).

Practicing anthropologists, caught up in the rituals of a respected academic profession in which they are endeavoring wholeheartedly to succeed, are unlikely to see their own field with the detachment that characterizes Catherine's view of hers. And so it is not surprising that Pym cannot use practicing anthropologists as the sources of the anthropological scrutiny of the profession itself that *Less Than Angels* contains. What she does instead is to employ three characters, who are all anthropologists by training, but who for various reasons have not been completely absorbed into their profession, as vehicles for the novel's humorous observations concerning the odd customs of the anthropological world.

Mark Penfold and Digby Fox, third-year anthropology students, are somewhat detached from their profession by the mere fact of their youth. Since, as students, they have not yet earned a place in the anthropological establishment, they observe it with the ironic distance of outsiders. Finding themselves, by an unusual accident, present at an anthropological cocktail party to which they were not invited, Mark and Digby stand, with symbolic discomfort, on the fringes of the crowd and study its rituals. " 'Dear boy! My *dear* Felix, my *dear* Gervase,' [says] Mark scornfully" (210), as he hears the professors present addressing one another in this intimate manner. "It's an interesting study when you come to consider it," Digby replies thoughtfully, "the lower you are in status, the more formal the type of address used, unless you're a servant, perhaps" (21). In the course of the novel, Mark decides to leave anthropology, but Digby doesn't and we can see him losing some of his detachment from his profession as he begins to succeed and find his niche.

As much detached by his age as Digby and Mark originally were by their youth is the retired Professor Felix Mainwaring, whose upper-class background and Balliol education further set him off from his fellow anthropologists. Felix has used the leisure retirement gives him to develop other interests. Asked by a visitor where he keeps his professional library, Felix replies,

"Anthropological books? . . . You won't find any in this house.
. . . I am an old man now, I can do very well without them.
They are not the kind of reading to see me into my grave.
. . . I find myself turning to Shakespeare and the Bible" (209).
From the broader perspective he now holds, Felix can observe
the curious rituals of anthropology with anthropological precision: "Academic toilers do not understand the art of being fashionably late," he tells his assistant, Miss Clovis, as they prepare
for the anthropological cocktail party mentioned above, " 'If
it says six o'clock on the invitation cards, you can be sure that
my colleagues will arrive at that time.' His forecast was accurate
and the hands of the library clock were barely pointing to six
when a mass of people seemed almost to hurl itself through
the door" (14). With the aid of Digby, Mark, and Felix, Pym
suggests in *Less Than Angels* that the anthropological profession
is a primitive culture with its own strange rituals.

But an anthropologist need not be detached from anthropology itself in order to see that entertaining results are obtained
when anthropological observation is focused upon many of the
rituals of "our so-called civilized society" (254), as a character
in *An Unsuitable Attachment* calls it. Several characters in *Less
Than Angels,* including both practicing anthropologists like Tom
Mallow, who have little distance concerning the profession itself,
and people like Miss Clovis, who are not trained anthropologists,
but have learned something from associating with them, prove
able to look anthropologically at their own culture. And in order
to demonstrate how fruitfully anthropological coolness and distance can be applied to the study of our own society and its
customs, Pym constructs this novel around three contrasting
English subcultures: the London world of Bohemian students,
writers, and aspiring academics, the suburban world of the comfortable, kindly, conventional middle classes, and the mixed
rural and London milieu of the decaying landed gentry. As
the novel's narrator and anthropologically inclined characters
move among these subcultures, they can see each of them as,
in its own way, a primitive society governed by unexamined
and often ludicrous traditions and embodying those traditions
in its own peculiar language. In examining her three "primitive"
English subcultures, Pym focuses her attention upon certain aspects of social behavior that have always been among her own

favorites and that have the additional advantage of being frequently studied by anthropologists: courtship, the relationships
between men and women, and sex roles. In each of these areas
she finds that many of our customs are curious indeed.

Compared to other Pym novels, *Less Than Angels* describes
an unusually large number of romances, and each of these romances occurs according to an appropriate, yet comic, set of
rituals. In Bohemian London the rituals are casual, ad hoc: Catherine and Tom meet on a Channel boat and she offers "to put
him up in her spare room" (26) since he has no place to stay.
Unprotected by their parents, young women in London fall
easy prey to male selfishness: the devoted women who live with
neurotic young anthropologists "might one day become their
wives, but . . . if they were thrown aside [they] would accept
their fate cheerfully and without bitterness. They had learned
early in life what it is to bear love's burdens, listening patiently
to their men's troubles and ever ready at their typewriters should
. . . even a short article get to the stage of being written down"
(49).

This is courtship in London; in the suburbs, where young
people are more closely watched by their elders, a more protective courtship ritual has developed. Men and women meet at
the club, which, Dierdre thinks, differs from the African men's
associations of which she has read only in that "the object of
many of these seemed to be to intimidate the women . . .
whereas here women were allowed to belong to some sections
of the club and might even be considered as one of its amenities"
(40). The men serve the women sweet gin drinks and take
them strolling by the river where, Tom reflects "in his detached
anthropologist's way" as he goes there with Dierdre, young
people "are allowed a certain amount of licence" (151). But
only a certain amount—visiting Tom's room in London, Dierdre
unconsciously follows the customs of her suburban background
when, "after a quick, nervous glance," and "for some reason
not quite clear to her" (141), she rejects the idea of sitting
down on his bed.

Whether living in the country or in London, the characters
from upper-class rural backgrounds follow a more formalized
and therefore funnier set of courtship rituals. Girls are exhibited
at dances and other artificial occasions, with the object of getting

them engaged as speedily as possible. Should a girl not look the part, there is despair in Belgravia. Tom's aunt is close to hysteria, "pretty desperate" (160), because her daughter Lalage "is five foot *eleven*" (137), and as she searches for suitable young men to invite to Lalage's coming out party—"the regular ones get so blasé and often don't turn up at all"—her first question about fresh prospects is invariably, "are they tall?" (136). So the reader heaves a sigh of relief when, at the end of the novel, Tom's sister announces that, "My cousin has just managed to get herself engaged, in her first season, too. Good show, isn't it?" (254).

Courtship practices differ in the novel's three locales, but the relationships between men and women tend in all of them— as in most of Pym's other work—to be characterized by exploitation of the latter by the former. Where so much else varies, this stays constant. Discussing, anthropologically, the "arrangement" whereby Tom and Catherine live together, Mark says, "it would be a reciprocal relationship—the woman giving the food and shelter and doing some typing for him and the man giving the priceless gift of himself. . . . It is commoner in our society than many people would suppose" (76). In suburbia, the unmarried Rhoda, answering a plea in the parish magazine, agrees to launder the albs of the local priest, Father Tulliver, whose wife has been ill. "It was so good of you to respond to my appeal. . . . I'm not much of a hand at laundering," Father Tulliver chuckles, "with the confidence of one who has never tried and does not intend to" (145). "Why couldn't Father Tulliver send them to the laundry, then?" (174) Dierdre asks when she sees the albs dripping in the kitchen on a rainy day. Rhoda doesn't know, but a man doesn't need irrefutable reasons in order to work effectively on a woman's guilt and her desire to serve. When Dierdre tells Rhoda scornfully, " 'Well, I certainly wouldn't do that for a man' . . . the typing she had sometimes done for Tom" (174), with whom she has fallen in love, conveniently slips her mind. In the country it's the same story. Tom's mother "loved him deeply, indulging his whims and thinking by that to bind him more closely to her" (178). But her strategy has failed dramatically; her son's visits home are few and brief.

Social conventions concerning "suitable" masculine and femi-

nine behavior are examined in the relationship that develops
between Catherine and the retired colonial administrator Alaric
Lydgate. In all of the novel's three locales some of the characters
rebel against traditional sex role expectations. In the anthropological circle in London, we find independent working women
like Catherine and Miss Clovis and even a great, dedicated
woman scholar, Alaric's sister Gertrude Lydgate. In Tom's rural
home, his mother, "a strong, active woman" (178), manages
the property, while his uncle passively watches television. And
in suburbia, Dierdre flees from the confined world of her mother
and aunt to study anthropology. So Pym begins by making it
clear that people from all sorts of backgrounds are sometimes
unable to conform to the generalized cultural expectation that
men be strong, productive, and protective, and women loving
and domestic. However, it is only in Alaric Lydgate that Pym
examines closely what will happen when a man who is radically
unsuited to it feels he must play the conventional role assigned
to his sex—and through this characterization she implies, as
she does in several of her novels, that men, rather than women,
are the worst victims of the sexist society she portrays.

The middle-aged "Alaric Lydgate regarded himself as a failure. He had been invalided out of the colonial service, where
he had not been awarded the promotion he felt he had earned"
(57–58). Since it is important to men to be healthy and competent and to have their competence acknowledged and rewarded,
Alaric feels he has failed as a man. His one chance to redeem
himself resides, he thinks, in writing up the notes he has taken
on the tribe whose affairs he administered and thus becoming
recognized as an anthropologist and linguist. But somehow he
cannot bring himself to undertake this work "and the trunks
of notes up in his attic, which he had never even sorted out,
were a constant reproach to him" (58).

Alaric has several defense mechanisms for dealing with his
sense of the disparity between what a man ought to be and
what he himself is. One of these is to hide his sense of failure,
figuratively and also literally, behind a mask. Seen on ordinary
occasions he wears a "grim expression" that makes his face
reminiscent of "images from Easter Island" (92)—in short, he
tries to look like the strong silent type of popular fiction, the
sort of man who may not say much about his work, but will

surely write up his field notes one day or another. When he is alone, however, Alaric often finds the Easter Island persona an insufficient defense against the generalized social scrutiny and contempt he fears from others—and also feels toward himself—and on these occasions he hides his face "under [an African] mask of red beans and palm fibre . . . withdrawing himself from the world" (57). Only while wearing his mask does Alaric feel safe in letting his face assume a natural expression and he "often thought what a good thing it would be if the wearing of masks or animals' heads could become customary. . . . How restful social intercourse would be if the face did not have to assume any expression" (57). What Alaric is hiding behind the mask is his sense of "feminine" ineffectuality. On evenings when it is too hot to wear the mask, he feels "defenceless, as if people passing could look in through the window and see him sitting there idle" (93), as a woman might do. Retiring long after midnight, he sets his alarm clock for six, as if he had to leave for work.

Alaric's other defense against his feeling of failure is to lash out in sarcastic reviews against more productive scholars—he is no exception to the generalization that frustration and insecurity often take the form of aggression. Alaric's desire to cut other scholars down to his own size is comic in its intensity. Slashing an anthropological study to pieces, Alaric gets so carried away that he begins three successive paragraphs with the phrase, "It is a pity," and cannot resist remarking, with hostile redundancy, that the learned society that funded the study had "squandered to no purpose" its limited resources (59).

"Like so many men, [Alaric] needed a woman stronger than himself, for behind the harsh cragginess of the Easter Island facade cowered a small boy, uncertain of himself" (242), says the narrator—and Alaric is lucky indeed to find Catherine. Detached and critical in her view of the social norms that others accept unthinkingly, Catherine can show Alaric that he need not spend the rest of his life in misery because he is unable to succeed as an anthropologist or to conform to society's ideal of what a man should be.

For Catherine the sort of imaginative literature often written by women is superior to the serious social science that is largely the property of men, but Alaric originally takes the opposite

view. When Catherine tells him that she is writing a story about
a retired big game hunter and that she wants to know if "the
thoughts about the country he's been in," which she has put
into his head, are "too wildly improbable" (155), Alaric is quick
to assert that he cannot help her because he possesses none of
the "feminine" quality of imagination: "I shouldn't like to say
what thoughts might be in the mind of a big game hunter,"
(155), he retorts stiffly. When he asks Catherine how her story
will end, Alaric is careful to smile in a superior manner "as if
he were humoring a child" (155), making it clear that he has
no real interest in the question. It soon becomes apparent to
Catherine that he is completely ignorant of even the most standard conventions of romantic fiction. Because he simply takes
the value of anthropological work for granted, Alaric is quite
surprised at Catherine's response when he consults her about
the problem of his field notes. "But . . . do you have to write
up the material?" she asks him, "wouldn't it be rather a bore
to have to do it?" (224). At this suggestion Alaric "could think
of absolutely nothing to say. . . . He felt as if the ground were
slipping away from under his feet. . . . But suddenly the sun
broke through on the grim surface of the carved rock and he
smiled. 'But what should I *do* with all my notes if I didn't write
them up?' he asked. 'Oh, we'd soon think of something,' said
Catherine gaily" (224).

Under Catherine's tutelage Alaric can escape from the idea
that his life will be justified only by significant achievement,
can learn to smile playfully and enter the "feminine" world
of imagination. And so, on Guy Fawkes night, Alaric and Catherine, wearing masks and African robes, dance round the bonfire
on which they are burning his notes. To celebrate Alaric's freedom from the conventions that have caused him so much pain,
they violate one more norm and invite his housekeeper to join
them in a glass of wine, though "the idea of drinking with
Mrs. Skinner was certainly a startling one" (228). The potential
social value of the notes is converted to real aesthetic value as
the burning paper "eaten by white ants, fell away like a shower
of confetti. 'Oh, pretty,' Catherine cried" (229). Arriving coinci-
dentally on the scene, Miss Clovis rescues a half-burned sheet
that says, "They did not know when their ancestors left the
place of the big rock nor why, nor could they say how long

they had been in their present habitat" (228). If this sample is representative of Alaric's notes, they may indeed be more valuable in the burning than they would have been if he had managed to write them up.

When he is asked by his sister what he will do next, Alaric declares his allegiance to Catherine's values: "I shall be free to do whatever I want to. I shall still review books . . . but I could even write a novel, I suppose" (229). Perhaps, since Alaric has "the most wonderful material" (229)—his observations of African life—and now is starting to use his imagination as well, the novel he writes will, like *Less Than Angels* itself, incorporate rather than reject the teachings of anthropology. As his decision to continue reviewing anthropological books shows, Alaric is not giving up anthropology completely, but he is refusing to justify his existence solely by success in fields of endeavor whose practitioners are mostly male. In this respect his decision to write fiction differs from a similar decision made by the heroine of Pym's last novel, *A Few Green Leaves*—for her choice, as we shall see in chapter 5, implies a real rejection of social science.

Anthropology and linguistics are related disciplines and so it is not surprising that in her "anthropological" study of the three social worlds in which her novel is set, Pym should give some attention to the language in which each subculture embodies its peculiar worldview. The London subculture of anthropologists tends, at least in its writing, toward pomposity and jargon, but apart from anthropological jargon, this subculture speaks a language that is free, slangy, and rather frank, especially about sexual matters. "All that talk about celibacy was rather unnerving for you boys," (205) a woman fellow student tells Mark and Digby after an occasion at which it has been claimed that an anthropologist in the field should be "a dedicated being very much like a priest" (205). Suburbia, by contrast, is the land of euphemism. When Dierdre's mother approvingly calls a local boy "a high principled young man," Dierdre knows just what she means and answers immediately, "Yes . . . only the mildest of good-night kisses" (61). In a world where words are used to smooth out the rough edges of things, Catherine's playfully comic exaggerations mystify. Leaving Mabel and Rhoda's house, where she has been visiting since Tom's death, Catherine says, "Of course, I must get back to my own squalor, really—you

understand, don't you?" (249). But they don't because they
speak a different language and afterwards Rhoda remarks "to
Mabel that she couldn't understand why Catherine always referred to her living conditions in such strange terms" (249).
In the milieu of the decaying landed gentry, language itself
tends to be comically antiquated, decayed: "Many eyes will be
upon you. We are still the leading family here" (181), Tom's
brother admonishes him. His aunt remarks that she doesn't
"think that there should be different codes of behavior for men
and women, though of course that view *was* held, and in the
highest circles" (135).

Pym's "anthropological" approach in *Less Than Angels* demonstrates the comic, peculiar, and fascinating nature of the rituals,
customary beliefs, and language that everyone, as a member
of one culture or another, unconsciously accepts and uses—and
their resemblance to those of societies we think of as more
primitive than our own. Thus the narrator is only half in jest
when she calls a seminar "this barbarous ceremony, possibly a
throwback to the days when Christians were thrown to the lions.
. . . Somebody prepared and read a paper on a given subject,
after which everybody else took great pleasure in tearing it
and its author to pieces and contributed their own views on
various matters not always entirely relevant" (48).

Even where questions of religious belief are involved, primitive cultures do not necessarily prove inferior to our own. Thinking of Tom Mallow's accidental death in Africa, Esther Clovis
remembers the curious belief of an African tribe that "the dead
survive only as long as people think of them. When they are
forgotten, they die a second time and then reappear in the form
of small mushroom shaped anthills in the bush. This time they
are thought to be really dead. She began to wonder how long
she herself would be kept alive under these conditions" (246).
Initially this sounds bizarre, as others' beliefs usually do, but
in fact these strange ideas about death start Miss Clovis meditat-
ing in a way that is no less fruitful than the meditations evoked
in Catherine by the more familiar Western approach Vaughan's
lines express:

> He that hath found some fledg'd bird's nest, may know
>   At first sight if the bird be flown

But what fair Well, or Grove he sings in now
   That is to him unknown.

(242)

On reading this poem, Catherine "remembered the church she
had gone into [to pray for Tom's safety] . . . then the meeting
with the two pleasant faced women and the clergyman. . . .
Did *they* know, she wondered?" (242). Since there are no universally satisfactory answers to life's ultimate questions, the answers other cultures suggest are *all* of great interest, and so
an anthropological approach to culture can forward our understanding of the world, as it does in *Less Than Angels.* But in
none of her later work, as the next chapter will demonstrate,
does Pym again look on the social sciences with so sympathetically humorous an eye. Never again is she so willing to allow—
and to prove by the very structure of the novel she creates—
that the values and methods of anthropology and literature can
be combined, to the benefit of the latter.

A Glass of Blessings

Wilmet Forsyth, the beautiful, childless woman of thirty-three
who narrates *A Glass of Blessings,* feels that she is living an empty
and purposeless life. Wilmet's civil servant husband, Rodney,
no longer seems particularly excited by her presence. Financially
secure, she has not held a job for years, nor does she have
any domestic responsibilities in the elegant house she and Rodney share with his widowed mother, Sybil. And unlike many
other Pym heroines, Wilmet, though a pious woman, has never
taken up the church work that helps to organize their lives.
Wilmet's efforts first to escape from, and then to adjust to, her
situation provide the forward momentum for this uneventful
narrative.

The novel occurs during a period when Wilmet is becoming
increasingly involved with the life of St. Luke's, a local Anglo-
Catholic church that she has been attending for only a few
months when the story opens. Though Wilmet's growing sense
of belonging and even being needed at St. Luke's is carefully
documented, Wilmet herself is slow to see involvement with
the church as a potential solution to the problem of her aimless
life. Her thoughts, indeed, are running along different, though

equally conventional, lines: a love affair with an "interesting man" who "needs" her affection and understanding. Ironically it is in church, where Wilmet does ultimately find some help in her difficulties, that she first conceives the romantic interest that she mistakenly supposes will help her surmount them. During the service at St. Luke's, Wilmet catches sight of handsome Piers Longridge, brother of her friend Rowena Talbott. Wilmet does not know Piers very well, but now they talk and soon Wilmet and Sybil are attending Piers's evening classes in Portuguese, to learn a few useful phrases for a projected holiday.

At thirty-five, Piers is both an interesting and a pathetic figure. He has held many jobs, has never married in spite of his sister's efforts to put eligible girls in his path, and shows worrisome tendencies toward alcoholism. He is very different from Wilmet's sober and successful husband, Rodney, and unlike Rodney he appears to need help. So Wilmet is delighted when Piers makes overtures of friendship to her and though these overtures are in fact few and far between, she creates a fantasy whereby her friendship helps reform him and make him happy: "Piers really needed me as few people did . . . needed love and understanding, perhaps already he was happier for knowing me" (163). Wilmet has always enjoyed painting imaginary vignettes—reading in the Parish Magazine, for example, that the two St. Luke's priests need a new housekeeper immediately because they "can just about boil an egg" between them, she imagines "them at the stove anxiously watching the boiling water; then, watches in hand, lowering the eggs into the saucepan" (26). But here Wilmet's imagination gets out of hand. Though Wilmet is increasingly aware of the sexual element in her feeling for Piers, she distracts her own attention from it by focusing her thoughts on the altruistic aspects of her desire to get close to him, attempting to have her Christianity and her extramarital attachment, too.

In looking to Piers to provide an escape from her sense of uselessness, of being a superfluous woman in her own world, Wilmet is simply doing what the habits of a lifetime have taught her to do. Like that of other beautiful women in Pym's novels, such as Prudence in *Jane and Prudence,* who is mentioned in *A Glass of Blessings* and said to resemble Wilmet, or Leonore Eyre in *The Sweet Dove Died,* Wilmet's beauty has shaped her personality in various destructive ways. Used to receiving admiration for what she is, rather than for what she does, Wilmet has become a very passive woman and has developed something of an obsession with the admiration of men. She never really examines her assumption that her happiness is to be found in the romantic love her beauty can create. Thus Wilmet is so preoccupied with the possibility of finding a new love, that she fails to realize she is already a fairly happy woman whose happiness derives from sources which have little to do with beauty or romance. But unlike Pym's other beautiful heroines, Wilmet *is* finally able to escape from narcissism, for in the end she realizes that friendships with women, the church, and marital affection are really more important to her than the romantic love she has been seeking.

Because Wilmet believes that love is the tribute paid to beauty, she is, for an intelligent woman, extraordinarily slow to notice the love affairs of her less than beautiful female friends. On her way to take tea with Piers, Wilmet sees "a drab-looking woman in a tweed skirt and crumpled pink blouse" and feels "suddenly embarrassed" and guilty as she thinks of the hopeless life so plain a woman *must* lead: "What could her life have held? What future was there for her?" (189). Because she sees love as a tribute paid to loveliness, Wilmet misinterprets the clearest signs that her stocky, nondescript, sixty-nine-year-old mother-in-law, Sybil, is developing a romantic relationship with an old friend, Professor Root, and the announcement of their engagement—preceded though it is by such conventionally romantic signs as gifts of long-stemmed roses—takes her completely by surprise.

Wilmet also misinterprets the love affair that develops between her dowdy friend Mary Beamish, a tireless worker for various good causes, and the extraordinarily good-looking assistant priest of St. Luke's, Father Marius Ransome. Although Mary confides to Wilmet virtually every forward step in their relationship—from Marius's asking her to call him by his first name, to his sharing with her his doubts concerning the validity of Anglican orders—Wilmet simply assumes that any feeling plain Mary has for gorgeous Marius must be hopeless and one-sided: "If he . . . decided to marry, he would choose somebody younger and more attractive than Mary" (164). So when this most

predictable engagement is announced, Wilmet is still capable
of feeling "astonishment that such a good-looking man as Marius
Ransome should want to marry anyone so dim and mousy"
(228), though it is perfectly clear to her that Mary will make
an ideal clergyman's wife. Wilmet must learn how complex an
emotion love is, and how many forms it can take.

Fixated upon conventional ideas of romantic love, Wilmet
fails to notice what is really important in her own life. In addition
to her "love" for Piers, Wilmet briefly considers both Marius
Ransome and Harry Talbott, the husband of her best friend,
Rowena, as possible admirers. With just a few intimate smiles
and a few pleasantries that seem, because of their tinge of cyni-
cism, a bit indiscreet in a clergyman, Marius manages to make
Wilmet feel that he has a special interest in her. She finds it
"galling to think of him living at the Beamishes," where he
has rented a room, because "no doubt Mary would adopt a
kind of proprietary attitude to him" (61). But it is really Wilmet,
not Mary, who sees Marius as to some extent her own property,
though she has no possible use to which she can put him. Marius
does little except look the part to encourage Wilmet's interest,
but Harry Talbott certainly does make several crudely sexual
overtures to her. Though Wilmet has no intention of respond-
ing—she doesn't find Harry very attractive and, in any case,
he is a good deal like Rodney—his admiration gives her a
"pleased and comfortable feeling" (47). As in her relationship
with Piers, so also with Harry, Wilmet convinces herself that
her pleasure in his advances is motivated by altruism: "I could
show Harry what a good wife Rowena was . . . it seemed an
excellent winter programme" (47).

While Wilmet is thinking about Piers, Marius, and Harry,
none of whom really means much to her, she is ignoring relationships, most of them with women, that are an important part
of her daily life. The first of these is her developing friendship
with Mary Beamish, which is quite explicitly paralleled, throughout the novel, with her relation to Piers. Originally, Wilmet
finds earnest, eager, self-sacrificing Mary, pillar of the church
and slave of a capricious invalid mother, both annoying and
threatening. "Mary Beamish was the kind of person who always
made me feel particularly useless," Wilmet thinks, seeing Mary
at a charitable committee meeting where she herself has gone

only to keep Sybil company, but where Mary's presence is vital, "she was so very much immersed in good works, so *splendid,* everyone said. . . . This particular morning, which seemed to me in my nastiness the last straw, she had just been to a blood donor session and had apparently come away sooner than she ought to have done" (47). In spite of Wilmet's persistent dislike, however, Mary begins to seek her out and without Wilmet's really noticing it, a friendship grows between them.

The reason Mary seeks Wilmet out, though they are so different, is Marius Ransome. In her daily round of good works, Mary meets few fashionable, pretty women who appear to have experienced a side of life of which Mary knows nothing, but of which, having met Marius, she would like to know more. And so Mary asks Wilmet to advise her about buying a new dress. As she tries to convince Mary that black will suit her better than the nondescript blues and greens she usually favors, Wilmet wonders "why I was taking all this trouble over Mary Beamish, for when one came to think of it, what did it matter what she wore?" (80).

In spite of Wilmet's hostile desire to keep Mary in her place, an attractive dress and some frivolous pink pearls are selected, but later, at tea, when Mary begins to quote poetry as a prelude to an intimate chat, Wilmet's irritation becomes unmanageable. "I felt I could not bear to be invited to a womanly sharing of confidences. I . . . saw almost with dislike her shining, eager face, her friendship offered me. What was I doing sitting here with somebody who was so very much not my kind of person? . . . I was unable to decide what it was that I found so irritating about her goodness; it could not only be that she was such a contrast to myself and made me feel guilty and useless" (84). Oversimplified as this explanation of Wilmet's hostility to Mary may sound, it is the correct one—and in the problem, the solution is found. As it becomes evident that Mary truly needs her, Wilmet no longer feels useless when she is around Mary and the friendship becomes a source of satisfaction to her. However, Wilmet hardly notices this happiness because of her preoccupation with Piers, whom she imagines to need her in precisely the way that Mary really does.

At Christmas Wilmet receives two unexpected presents. The first is a gift of handkerchiefs from Mary, to whom Wilmet has given nothing because "we've never exchanged presents before" (105). Mary's attempt to mark an advance in their relationship goes unnoticed, for at the time Wilmet is "really thinking of [another] present" (105), a little Victorian enamel box with the inscription, "If you will not when you may / When you will you shall have nay," which has arrived anonymously in the mail. Wilmet believes that Piers sent her the box as a joking reference to an evening when she was forced to turn down his spur-of-the-moment invitation to dinner, and she takes the box as proof of his special feeling for her. Actually, as Wilmet will later learn, the box comes from Harry Talbott and is a fairly crude allusion to her cool reception of his advances. As with Mr. Elton's charade in *Emma*—another novel of an imaginative heroine who invents unreal romances and overlooks real ones, and a novel to which Barbara Pym sometimes compared *A Glass of Blessings* when discussing her own work[1]—so here, a romantic overture is grossly misinterpreted. In her preoccupation with Piers's supposed Yuletide gesture, Wilmet overlooks the real change in her relationship with Mary that occurs when Mary's tyrannical mother suddenly dies on the day after Christmas. Moved by the spectacle of her usually splendid, self-sacrificing friend feeling lost because she no longer needs to organize her life around her mother's demands, Wilmet tries to comfort Mary and unconsciously ceases to find her irritating.

Mary decides to enter an Anglican convent and one spring afternoon Wilmet lunches with Piers before going to call on her. At lunch Wilmet makes Piers a vague offer of help in his troubles and his offhand response, "You're very sweet" (163), puts her into an exalted mood that has little foundation in reality. But arriving at the convent, Wilmet finds a situation in which she really can be useful: Mary desperately wants to tell her about some disturbing letters she has received from Marius, for Mary thinks of Wilmet as a woman who knows a lot about men. Mary also tells Wilmet that she has decided to leave the convent and Wilmet invites Mary to stay with her while deciding what to do next.

On the day Mary arrives for her visit, Wilmet again has a date with Piers, quite a coincidence in view of how seldom she sees either Piers or Mary. Feeling like a young girl in love, Wilmet goes to take tea with Piers at his flat and makes a horrifying discovery: the "colleague" with whom she has imagined Piers to share his flat is really a beautiful, working-class youth named Keith. Piers is a homosexual and the contented frame of mind he has lately been in is not to be attributed, as Wilmet believed, to her own "charms and loving care" (200), but rather to the care and charms of the kindly, loyal, domestic Keith. Returning home in a state of deep "humiliation and disappointment" (200)—and the use of the word "humiliation" here again reminds the reader of *Emma,* where the same term describes the heroine's feeling on coming to perceive how generally mistaken about the world she has been—Wilmet finds that Mary has arrived. "I shall really have to do some shopping," Mary tells her, "I've no summer things. Will you help me, Wilmet, please?" And Wilmet thinks, "I saw us shopping together, having lunch or tea in a restaurant. . . . I knew that time would pass and I should feel better" (201). The ways in which Mary needs Wilmet are not as spectacularly satisfying as the ways in which she imagined Piers to need her, but now that Wilmet is no longer preoccupied with her imaginary romance, she can see that Mary's friendship is a source of satisfaction: "I was glad in the days that followed to have Mary with me" (205).

Wilmet's friendship with Rowena Talbott, a woman very similar to herself, also proves to have a greater significance for Wilmet than she initially realized. Rowena has always been Wilmet's best friend, but in the course of the novel Wilmet comes to understand how much she cares for Rowena. Most of the time, Rowena and Wilmet's friendship is expressed in trivial activities like going to the hairdresser together and examining one another's clothes and nails, but there is a deeper rapport between them as well. It is Rowena who tells Wilmet that Harry bought the little box Wilmet supposed to come from Piers. Rowena explains to Wilmet how she came to know about the box and the two women have a frank and pleasant discussion of the "bit of a thing" (137) Harry has for Wilmet. Rowena's calm reaction to her husband's crush on her best friend impresses Wilmet deeply, and so Harry's attempts to get closer to Wilmet actually have the effect of bringing her closer to Rowena emotionally and, ironically, in a physical sense as well: "We linked arms and went down to join the men. I reflected what a splendid and wonderful thing the friendship of really nice women was.

It could surely be said that Rowena and I were fortunate in each other" (137). Earlier in the novel it was Harry who surreptitiously held Wilmet's hand—now Rowena holds it openly.

The third woman about whom Wilmet must come to understand her feelings is her mother-in-law, Sybil. In the other two paired relationships—with Piers and Mary, and with Harry and Rowena—Wilmet must learn that though she thinks she is interested in the man, she really feels more for the woman. The problem with Sybil, however, is somewhat different, for this relationship is paired with Wilmet's relationship to her husband, Rodney, who, because of Wilmet's preoccupation with the romantic love that marriage cannot provide, might be called the forgotten man in her life. Here Wilmet must come to realize the degree to which she depends upon Sybil for companionship and emotional sustenance, some of which, at least, she could be getting from her husband. Wilmet learns that she and Rodney should move closer to one another, but she cannot do this until she acknowledges how important Sybil has been to her.

It is clear to the reader, if not to Wilmet herself, that Sybil is one of the main reasons that Wilmet has been able to tolerate her life with Rodney. There is a fair amount of friction between irrepressible Sybil and sober Rodney. He is constantly throwing her warning glances and making irritable remarks of the "surely, Mother, you aren't thinking . . ." (15) variety—when, for example, Sybil suggests jokingly that they might turn their house into a rehabilitation home for Anglican priests who have been defrocked for seducing the boys in their youth clubs. But the relationship between Sybil and Wilmet is completely unruffled. Sybil worries about Wilmet's creature comforts and tries to make her feel valued—it is she, for example, and not Rodney, who chooses a special birthday dinner for Wilmet. She tries to keep Wilmet busy, but tactfully avoids saying anything that might imply criticism of Wilmet's aimless life. Wilmet responds with sincere affection and admiration for Sybil, whom she finds extremely amusing.

Wilmet's relationship with Rodney, on the other hand, though certainly not a bad one, has failed to maintain the solid emotional reality that characterizes her response to Sybil. It's easy to see *A Glass of Blessings* as just another novel about an intelligent, pretty woman married to a dull or unappreciative man, as the jacket copy of the Harper & Row edition of the novel seems to do when it says that Wilmet is "bored with her excessively sober civil servant husband."[2] But, in fact, there is no great discrepancy between Rodney and Wilmet. Her pursuits and interests are as conventional for a woman as his are for a man. He is not unattractive, nor is he less intelligent or even less interesting than she. Indeed, both like to observe small details of human behavior and they share a similar quiet sense of humor. Visiting the St. Luke's Clergy House for the first time, Wilmet and Rodney are both interested in speculating about such matters as the original purpose of the room now used as an oratory—leaving, both "burst out laughing" (116) simultaneously as they remember the odd behavior of their host.

What is wrong between Wilmet and Rodney has more to do with the general difficulties of relationships between men and women than with any incompatibility between them as individuals. Rodney is a familiar male type from the recent past, primarily interested in his work, liking shoptalk more than other forms of conversation, and preferring that his wife not hold a job, if only to prove that he can support her in idleness. Wilmet, as we have seen, is an equally familiar type of nonworking woman, interested in clothes, men, and religion. So in spite of a basic temperamental suitability between them, Wilmet and Rodney go their semiseparate ways and their marriage ceases to be a great source of satisfaction to either. Further, since both have conventional ideas about the joys of romantic love, it is natural that the prosaic experience of marriage should disappoint them and that their thoughts should stray to other romantic possibilities.

At the end of the novel, however, Wilmet and Rodney are able to improve their marriage, at least to some degree. The catalyst for this development is Sybil's announcement that she is going to marry Professor Root. Two drastic changes in Wilmet's life follow: Sybil and Professor Root will go to Portugal alone on their honeymoon, instead of taking a family trip there with Wilmet and Rodney, and when they return they want to live by themselves in Sybil's house. So Wilmet and Rodney must go on vacation à deux and then set up housekeeping, apparently the first time they will have lived alone together in ten years. At first these prospects dismay Wilmet. Her "heart rather sank" (222) as Rodney makes plans for a trip to Cornwall and she suddenly realizes "how much [she] should miss [Sybil]" (221) when they no longer live together. Only their approaching separation makes Wilmet aware of the degree to which she has relied on Sybil to be, emotionally, a substitute for Rodney.

Vacationing alone in rain-swept Cornwall and looking for a place to live force Wilmet and Rodney to communicate and bring them "closer together than we had been for years" (247). Rather surprisingly, it is Rodney, and not Wilmet, who initiates an intimate discussion of the state of their marriage, probably the first they have had in a long while. He confesses to Wilmet that he has taken another woman—actually none other than Prudence Bates of *Jane and Prudence*—out to dinner several times. Hearing this, Wilmet realizes that she and Rodney have more in common than she had realized: "At the time when I had been occupied with foolish thoughts of Piers, my husband had been taking the attractive friend of a woman civil servant out to dinner. . . . I had always regarded Rodney as the kind of man who would never look at another woman. The fact that he could—and had indeed done so—ought to teach me something" (249–50). To make Rodney feel better, Wilmet tells him that she has had a few lunches with other men, and his instant response, "Lunch, yes. But dinner *is* rather different somehow" (250), with its complacent insistence that he is a bigger sinner, a gayer dog, than she, soon has them both giggling.

Not a very dramatic rapprochement, but enough to remind Wilmet that, though marriage is simply not the same thing as the romantic love she has been craving, her marriage to Rodney has its positive side—and Sybil's absence will help develop this side by forcing Wilmet and Rodney to take more thought for one another. But this does not imply that Wilmet is terminating her close relationship with Sybil, which remains extremely important to her. One might expect that a novel about a bored wife's dreams of romance would end in either of two ways: with affairs and the eventual destruction of the marriage, or with an affirmation of the marriage as central to her life. But *A Glass of Blessings* uses neither of these definitive, dramatic resolutions.

What Wilmet comes to realize is exactly what the novel's

title implies: that all along her life has been filled with blessings, of which her marriage is only one and not necessarily even the most important. Wilmet finds satisfaction in her friendships with women, her nice clothes and good looks, the passing admiration of men, her faculty for observation, her marriage, and her faith in God and growing involvement with the church. For, thanks to her friendship with Mary, Wilmet has found it "easy . . . to enter the charmed circle" (206) of church workers at St. Luke's, which earlier she had wished, but been somehow unable, to join. Wilmet's interest in everything connected with St. Luke's has steadily increased throughout the novel, so it seems clear that church work will be one of the ways she can deal with the sense of purposelessness that has bothered her so much.

Wilmet does not learn her lesson about the insufficiency of romantic love so thoroughly as to give up her interest in men, or in clothes, altogether, nor given the qualified nature of Pym's endings would we expect her to. She never becomes an excellent woman in the style of Mildred Lathbury or of Mary Beamish, though she moves in that direction. Even after her disappointment in Piers, Wilmet is still able to take comfort from the admiration her beauty excites, feeling, for example, "well satisfied" when she catches Harry Talbott "looking at me with a kind of doggy devotion in his eyes" (215). But she is now able to see that this particular source of pleasure cannot continue to be at the center of her life. Wilmet is by no means totally chastened by her mistake about Piers and there is really no reason that she should be. She did not need to change radically, but rather to put her life in perspective, to see it as a whole. And so the concluding lines of the novel stress Wilmet's diverse sources of happiness. Returning from attending Marius's induction into his new church, Wilmet "turned into the street where our new flat was, and where I knew Rodney would be waiting for me. We were to have dinner with Sybil and Arnold that evening. It seemed a happy and suitable ending to a good day" (256).

Chapter Five

The Later Novels

The Sweet Dove Died

The Sweet Dove Died returns, in a grimmer mood, to a character type that had figured prominently in two of the novels Pym wrote during the fifties: the woman whose great beauty has proved an obstacle to the development of her ability to love. Wilmet Forsyth does manage in the course of *A Glass of Blessings* to overcome the emotional problems her beauty has created, but Prudence Bates in *Jane and Prudence* ultimately finds herself unable to renounce the excitements of flattery and admiration in favor of a stable relationship. Even Prudence's vanity, however, looks mild when it is compared to the narcissism of Leonora Eyre, the heroine of *The Sweet Dove Died.* For Prudence, though selfish and affected in her dealings with others, hurts no one but herself by her childish antics and retains a saving affection for her likable friend Jane. Leonora's narcissism, however, is too destructive to be amusing in the way that Prudence's rather harmless vanity certainly was.

An extraordinarily lovely spinster in her late forties or early fifties, Leonora resembles Prudence in more than her good looks. Both women are extremely well groomed, more interested in possessions than in people, addicted to flattery, incapable of emotional generosity, and totally unsuited to marriage. But Leonora's values are far more purely and dramatically aesthetic than are Prudence's. Prudence's sense of herself is derived, to some extent, from her possessions, but Leonora identifies her very being with the objects that surround her, saying things like "Victoriana . . . somehow I feel they're me" (23), or, "Virginia Water. All those trees and distant ruins, so much *me*" (48).

Leonora thinks of herself as if she were a beautiful object, dependent for its full aesthetic success upon the proper setting.

Visiting a dingy women's club, the sort of place she does not ordinarily frequent, Leonora wonders, "How could people bear such places? One really felt most unlike oneself in surroundings like that" (187). She can reestablish her sense of her own reality only by placing herself again in a suitable setting and so, leaving the club, she "found herself entering [Fortnum and Mason's]. She wanted to feel the soft carpets under her feet and to move among jars of foie gras and bottles of peaches in brandy" (187). In fact, Leonora's detached sense of herself as an object to be contemplated from the outside and evaluated in purely aesthetic terms has become completely habitual, so that she characteristically thinks of herself as "one," rather than as "I": "One was not at one's best in the rain, obviously" (155), and so forth. Leonora also has a devouring passion for perfect objects. She "liked things to be flawless, expected them to be" (75). "She could not bear to have anything not quite perfect in the room" (201).

Even Leonora's imagination is stimulated primarily by things rather than by people. A "favorite diversion" for evenings spent with an intimate is "reading [aloud] from sale catalogues . . . the seductive descriptions . . . brought the beautiful pieces before her eyes—narrow crossbandings of tulipwood, palm tree motifs, and eagles cresting . . ." (52). Sometimes it seems as if Leonora has forgotten that there is a difference between people and objects. When her friends' antique shop is burglarized, she sends "a sheaf of white roses and carnations tied with mauve ribbon" (72), accompanied by a message offering "sympathy in your sad losses" (73)—exactly what it would be proper to send after a death.

Leonora expects flawlessness in her possessions and, because she sees herself as an object, in her life too. And one result of this is her pathological fear of aging and death. A beautiful object, well cared for, need not decay, but a beautiful woman must, a fact Leonora simply cannot accept. Leonora's violent, ruthless hatred of the frail, elderly Miss Foxe, the tenant of an upper flat in her house, seems attributable only to her own fear of the ravages of time of which Miss Foxe is such a forcible reminder. For though Leonora tells herself that "there was no reason why one's death should not, in its own way, be as elegant as one's life" (18), the reader must view this assertion as a

shallow piece of self-deception. Aging and death are not elegant
processes, though they can, of course, be confronted with stoic
dignity.

And in fact, Leonora judges all actions, feelings, and relationships in terms of the way they either contribute to or detract
from the impression of elegance she wishes her life to produce,
subordinating to the aesthetic, both the sexual and the emotional, as well as the moral. *The Sweet Dove Died* is the frankest
of all Pym's novels in its treatment of sex, and the narrator
alludes quite explicitly to Leonora's sexual coldness. Thinking
back over her life, Leonora can recall no real passion, only
"one or two tearful scenes in bed—for she had never really
enjoyed *that* kind of thing—and now it was such a relief that
one didn't have to worry any more" (16). When an admirer,
Humphrey Boyce, kisses her passionately, Leonora panics and
tries to scream, "but no sound came," and she thinks resentfully
that "surely freedom from this sort of thing was among the
compensations of advancing age and the sad decay of one's
beauty" (92). At least a part of Leonora's dislike of sex seems
to derive from the indignity of it all: one's lacquered hair gets
ruffled and arrangement becomes impossible. One is even in
some danger of forgetting altogether about how one looks.
When Humphrey kisses her, Leonora's first thought is indeed
of this sort: "One couldn't lose one's dignity, of course" (92).

So Leonora's aestheticism seems to make sexuality impossible,
and it has equally dramatic effects in the realms of emotion
and personal relationships. The main focus of *The Sweet Dove
Died* is upon the friendship that develops between Leonora and
James Boyce, a handsome, but weak, antique dealer of twenty-
four, nephew of Leonora's friend and suitor, Humphrey.
Though she treats Humphrey pleasantly, Leonora, from the start,
prefers the platonic, sentimental relationship James offers her
to anything Humphrey can provide. And given her horror of
aging and death, it is clear that James's youth is an important
aspect of his attraction for Leonora.

Soon she and James are meeting nearly every day, Leonora
cooking James perfect little meals with the right wines, James
giving Leonora perfect little items from his shop and driving
her about in his car. James's good looks satisfy Leonora aesthetically and flatter her too, for she sees him as "the beautiful young

man with whom people were always falling in love and who yet remained inexplicably and deeply devoted to her, a woman so much older than he was" (51). James has recently lost the mother who raised him after his father's early death and is both shy and uncertain about his own sexual inclinations. For him a friendship with an older woman who will cherish him as his mother once did is obviously alluring and since he too is an aesthete, seeking beauty, order, and comfort in his surroundings, Leonora appeals to him as much as he does to her.

Does this odd relationship have a sexual side? As far as James is concerned, the answer seems to be no, but as it relates to Leonora the question is more difficult to answer. Sometimes it seems as though a part of James's attraction for Leonora is the impossibility that a real sexual relationship could develop between them, given their difference in age and James's curious passivity. She can stroke his hair and say, "How curly it is! Like golden wires or whatever the Elizabethan poets said" (140), without any fear that he will want to disarrange *her* hairdo in response. Thinking of Humphrey's aggressive kiss, Leonora reflects fondly that "dear James wouldn't expect anything like *that . . .*" (119). But at other times this seems less clear, as when Leonora finds it "amusing to toy with the idea of marrying James" (119). Thinking of her irritation at Humphrey's advances, Leonora more than once asks herself, "Would she have minded if it had been *James?*" (140). In Pym's work, sex always tends to be an area of confusion and self-delusion, and though more is said about Leonora's sexual impulses than about those of most other Pym characters, their nature remains irreducibly puzzling.

Nonetheless sex finally does spoil for Leonora the "perfect relationship" (142) with James, which is her most treasured possession. Unable or unwilling to become sexually involved with James herself, Leonora hopes to preserve him in the sexually unawakened state in which she found him, sensing that a lover might well take James away from her. But James, though passive and insecure, certainly does not resemble Leonora in being repelled by sex. Soon he becomes involved with Phoebe, an aggressive young girl who in many ways is Leonora's opposite. Sexually Phoebe is quite unrestrained—she seduces the very passive James on their second meeting. But while she offers

the lure of pure sexuality, which Leonora so totally lacks, Phoebe
is completely deficient in the sensual and aesthetic attractions
that are Leonora's strong points. Unlike Leonora, Phoebe has
no interest in clothes and refuses to define her identity through
beautiful objects: "Desirable Victoriana—not quite me" (43).
In her kitchen James notices "a cold joint standing on the table
. . . very much exposed to wandering animals . . . a bowl of
lettuce from which he surreptitiously removed a few inedible-
looking leaves which seemed to have earth adhering to them
. . . the washing up from lunch or breakfast or both, two un-
rinsed milk bottles, eggshells not thrown away, paw marks on
the sink and cats' hairs floating in the atmosphere" (64). Using
one of Leonora's favorite words, James decides that it would
not be "agreeable" to wake up in such an environment and
declines to stay for the night.

Partly because these sorts of aesthetic considerations are ultimately more important to James than sexual ones—just as they
are to Leonora—but partly also because his real sexual interest
is in men rather than in women, Leonora has little trouble detach-
ing James from Phoebe when their affair comes to her attention.
Faced with a choice between Phoebe's "raw outpouring of feelings" (107) and Leonora's ordered, controlled, elegant world,
James easily decides for the latter. But Ned, an American academic whom James meets while traveling in Portugal, proves
a more dangerous rival to Leonora precisely because he offers
the satisfactions of both sexuality and aestheticism.

Unlike Phoebe, who is plain, awkward, and very badly
dressed, Ned is handsome and possesses charm and style, which
immediately take "the centre of the stage" (151). In many ways
Ned is Leonora's male counterpart, but when they compete
he comes out ahead, "the glitter of his personality making [her]
seem no more than an ageing overdressed woman" (151). Like
Leonora, Ned has the vanity and emotional coldness fostered
by the possession of great beauty—"I've had to hurt people
so many times" (170), he tells James smugly, very much in
the manner of Fabian Driver. And Ned also resembles Leonora
in identifying himself with his possessions and surroundings,
saying things like "I do feel the bedroom's rather me" (157),
as he exhibits its decor. Since Ned offers nearly everything
that Leonora can offer, and sex as well, he easily detaches the

selfish and weak James from Leonora. Always eager to avoid a scene, James stops calling Leonora at Ned's insistence, just as he had previously stopped seeing Phoebe at Leonora's, and Leonora is left to deal with the humiliating, imperfect situation of having been rejected by the only person she really cares anything about.

Since Leonora has always placed aesthetic considerations first, it is not surprising that she immediately acts to preserve the beautiful, unruffled surface of her life by concealing from others and, as far as possible, from herself, the suffering she experiences. "A red face, working and blotched with tears" (199) is something both Ned and Leonora contemplate with distaste; pain, like sex, tends to be destructive of dignity and order. And so Leonora either hides from her friends the severity of the breach between James and herself, or pretends she does not care about it. And when James himself tries to explain why he acted as he did, Leonora assumes "a cool tone" and tells him, "I've never wanted to stop you from having your own friends—after all one isn't a monster" (172). Throughout the entire episode Leonora is "deliberately 'good' and 'understanding'" (162) in her treatment of James, never letting him see how hurt she feels. Finally the emotional dishonesty of this becomes too much even for James, who begins to wish "she would forget her dignity for a moment and make a scene" (162). Such a scene might well improve matters between them, since James really does care for Leonora in his fashion, but Leonora won't let her emotions escape from the control of her aesthetic sense enough to make it.

After losing James, Leonora tries to fall back on her other major source of satisfaction, beautiful possessions. "She had always cared as much for inanimate objects as for people and now spent hours looking after her possessions, washing the china and cleaning the silver obsessively. . . . Her love of beautiful objects led her again to make solitary excursions to the sale rooms" (182). Viewing Edwardian jewelry on one such occasion, Leonora finds herself beginning to cry "not only for herself, but also for the owners of the jewellery, ageing now or old, some probably dead" (183). Leonora goes to a grimy cafeteria to have some tea and pull herself together. While looking at her sordid surroundings, she becomes "conscious that she herself belonged here too with the sad jewellery and the old [waitress] and the air of things that had seen better days. Even the cast off crusts, the ruined cream cakes and the cigarette ends had their significance" (184).

At this point Leonora might well be humanized by her recognition of her own vulnerability, but instead she acts with instant determination to reject the powerful intimation of mortality she has experienced. She rigidly maintains her elegant composure with a distant cousin, Daphne, whom she meets soon afterwards and she firmly rejects a "desire to confide" her troubles to Daphne as an "absurd" (186) impulse. In this scene, Leonora seems to make her decision—if love has "debased, diminished, crushed" and brought her to the "point of dilapidation" (184) she feels herself to have reached in the cafeteria, she will have nothing further to do with it.

So it ought not to surprise readers that at the conclusion of the novel, it is Leonora who rejects James and not the other way round. The clever, sophisticated Ned has become bored with beautiful, but not very interesting James—lies, infidelities, and a final rupture between the two result. James, hurt and guilty, returns to Leonora, thinking that "Leonora would always be there, like some familiar landmark, like one's mother even" (205). But Leonora cannot accept this role. When James tells her of his rupture with Ned, Leonora is "aware that with this confidence she was receiving more from him than she ever had before, but unable to respond in the way that he obviously expected. She and James had both been hurt, but it hardly seemed to make a bond between them—it was more like a barrier or wedge driving them apart" (207).

The two wedges driving Leonora and James apart are Leonora's realization of the pain and indignity love can cause and the fact that she now views James, and her relationship with him, as damaged goods—given her love of perfection these things are fatal. James is no longer the irresistible, completely devoted young man to whom she can say "I wonder how many people have fallen in love with you today" (51), for now he is Ned's rejected lover and the cause of her own pain and humiliation. He has violated their "wonderful friendship" (199) once and clearly will do so again—and even though his affection for her could survive these betrayals, her affection for him cannot. No emotion which Leonora has felt or still feels toward James as an individual can outweigh her repugnance at tolerating an imperfect relationship with an imperfect young man and so she sends him away when he appears to seek a reconciliation, saying coolly "It was sweet of you to come" (208). As James leaves, Humphrey, appropriately, arrives to take Leonora to the Chelsea Flower Show where "the sight of such large and faultless blooms . . . was a comfort and satisfaction to one who loved perfection as she did" (208). Leonora has made her choice.

So, like Prudence Bates, Leonora ends up accepting and adjusting to the emotional limitations of her own narcissism. But where this commits Prudence to an endless series of superficial emotional involvements and ruptures, for Leonora it will mean the absence of any emotional involvement at all. On their first meeting, Ned quotes to Leonora from one of Keats's minor poems:

> I had a dove and the sweet dove died;
> And I have thought it died of grieving.
> O, what could it *grieve* for? Its feet were tied
> With a single thread of my *own hand's* weaving.
> (146)

Leonora sees the poem as having "some obscure and unpleasant meaning" (146). Clearly she sees herself as the speaker and James as the dove imprisoned, and perhaps finally to be destroyed, by the snare of the sensual and aesthetic delights she offers him, delights suggested by the artistically woven thread— and no less clearly, this is how Ned wants her to read the lines. The poem lingers in Leonora's mind when she sends James away at the end of the novel: "There was something humiliating about the idea of wooing James . . . like an animal being enticed back into his cage" (207). But the application of the poem to Leonora's situation is even more unpleasant than she realizes, for she herself is both speaker and dove. It is her own aesthetic approach to life that constricts and finally kills her emotionally— and she has chosen this imprisonment of her own free will.

The callous selfishness exhibited by several characters does a lot of emotional harm in *The Sweet Dove Died*. James hurts Phoebe and Leonora, Leonora and Ned hurt James, Leonora's

friend Meg suffers deeply from the neglect of her much loved
protégé Colin, while Leonora's neighbor Liz has been permanently scarred by a traumatic divorce. As in *Jane and Prudence,*
so here, selfishness is mostly male selfishness, but in *The Sweet
Dove Died* male selfishness is not the laughing matter it was in
the earlier novel, for it causes too much grief. When James
tells Leonora of his last "terrible scene" with Ned, in which
they found themselves "saying unforgivable things to each other
and throwing objects, such as . . . fur cushions . . ." (204),
Leonora is only briefly "tempted to laugh. It occurred to her
now that Ned was in many ways a comic character, but the
realization had come too late" (206). Leonora can see that Ned
is comic only *after* she has recovered from the terrible suffering
his vanity caused her, whereas Fabian, Ned's counterpart in
the earlier novel, was a comic character throughout, because
he did no real harm.

Like *Jane and Prudence, The Sweet Dove Died* is structured
around a series of contrasts between narcissistic characters and
characters who are able to love, and it darkens the latter novel's
tone considerably that all the characters who are capable of
real love are minor characters, whose love manifests itself in
less than completely satisfactory forms. Jane and Nicholas, in
the earlier novel, are rather eccentric people, but their conjugal
and parental love is of a *far* more pleasant and ordinary sort
than the loves of Leonora's friends.

Throughout the novel, Leonora's relationship to James is compared to the relationship between another middle-aged woman,
Meg, and another young homosexual, Colin. Meg, emotionally
unreserved, completely without aesthetic sense, and very generous, could hardly be more different from Leonora, who probably
tolerates her because she is such a perfect foil. Where Leonora's
involvement with James is motivated by the not very savory
impulses discussed earlier, Meg's interest in Colin is purely ma-
ternal. She needs to be needed and Colin is something of a
mess: emotionally unstable, in constant romantic turmoil, frequently unemployed. But as Leonora is quick to notice, the
excess of Meg's affectionate generosity tends to make her ridiculous, for Leonora is right when she tells Meg that Colin is truly
a "very selfish young man" (31) who comes around when he
needs Meg's sympathy and ignores her when he has other fish

to fry. When Colin callously fails to call her, Meg appears at Leonora's door in a state of near hysteria: she "looked a sight . . . in a dusty black polo sweater and baggy green corduroy trousers. Her hair was standing out in a bush and her face was red and swollen and streaked with tears. Leonora averted her gaze as she handed her a glass of whiskey—how could she bear to be seen in such a state?" (30).

Meg is willing to forgive Colin no matter how often he hurts her and she makes no particular attempt to conceal the humiliating terms of their relationship from her other friends. "If things seem to go wrong sometimes, we mustn't *stop* loving, that's the point as I see it" (165), she tells Leonora. Perhaps Meg might have found a more considerate recipient for her love than the selfish, disorganized Colin, but the basic problem would still remain: to love another human being is to expose yourself to pain, rejection, humiliation. Alone among the novel's characters, Meg decides to take this risk, and this gives her, as the narrator remarks, "a touch of pathos, even nobility" (166), in spite of the fact that she has not perhaps shown the best judgment in choosing Colin as the object of her love.

Deeply wounded by a bad marriage and traumatic divorce, Leonora's friend Liz simply cannot recover from the pain she has experienced. Every time Leonora visits her "Liz would embark again on the subject of her unhappy marriage. 'All that love, *wasted,*' she would say" (58). Unwilling to expose herself to further rejection and suffering, Liz is also unable to live a completely loveless life, and so she has become passionately devoted to the Siamese cats she breeds—for the cats, obviously, are unable to do her the emotional harm that another human being well might. So Leonora seems at least partly right to pity Liz and to reflect that "one would hardly want to be like the people who fill the emptiness of their lives with an animal" (188)—because to do so is clearly an admission that one has failed with other human beings. Liz's compromise is safe, but from Leonora's viewpoint nearly as unsatisfactory and humiliating as the course Meg has chosen.

During the period when Leonora is still suffering acutely over James's desertion, she loses control and cries only once, and this very brief lapse occurs, appropriately, in Meg's presence. "They always come back in the end," Meg tells Leonora consolingly, "You mustn't expect things to be perfect" (202). And *The Sweet Dove Died* does indeed imply that if you want to go on loving, as Meg and Liz do, you must be willing to accept exploitation, rejection, humiliation, or at least compromise— imperfection of all sorts. Since Leonora feels that "all one's relationships had to be perfect of their kind" (56–57), she is unable to do this and so must embrace the dignified, but frozen, narcissism that seems to be the only alternative offered by this uncharacteristically dark novel. Leonora sees her alternatives clearly, makes her choice with her eyes open, and so wins a kind of victory in the end. But in describing Leonora's final "triumph" over James in one of her literary notebooks, Pym wrote that "it is a Pyrrhic victory,"[1] and clearly this is also true. It makes the novel even sadder that Meg's and Liz's victories are Pyrrhic as well. *The Sweet Dove Died* is Pym's most pessimistic, but perhaps also her most touching, view of the humiliating extremes to which people must sometimes go in order to satisfy their need for "something to love."

Quartet in Autumn

Quartet in Autumn takes place in a London where the institutions that have traditionally related people to one another are no longer functioning, and where individuals find themselves isolated, unable to depend on others for companionship and aid. The quartet of protagonists to which the novel's title refers—Letty Crowe, Marcia Ivory, Edwin Braithwaite, and Norman (whose last name we do not learn)—are coworkers on the verge of retirement who share a common office and jointly form the staff of one small department in a large company. Because the department does almost no work, the narrator comments that for its employees "to clear one's desk" is "a phrase from long ago that had little or no reality in their present situation" (94). And in fact "the whole department [is] being phased out" (102) as its employees reach retirement age. The four employees of this superfluous department receive little satisfaction from their work. After her retirement Letty even asks herself if "what cannot now be justified has perhaps never existed, and it gave her the feeling that she and Marcia [who had retired at the same time] had been swept away as if they had never been" (114).

Relationships with family, friends, and neighbors, which might be expected to provide purpose and meaning when work fails to satisfy, are unable to do so in the fragmented world of *Quartet in Autumn.* Personal ties here are rare, unsatisfactory, and easily broken. Of the novel's four protagonists only Edwin, now a widower, has ever married or had a child. Edwin recalls his marriage without perceptible nostalgia—in a train station he sees "a colourful range of magazines on the counter, some of which displayed the full, naked breasts of young women, enticingly posed. Edwin looked at them dispassionately. He supposed that his wife Phyllis had once had breasts, but he could not remember that they had been at all like this" (45). Edwin's relationship with his daughter and grandchildren is marked by a similar feeling of distance and disjunction: "In the train coming back from staying with his daughter and her family, Edwin felt drained and exhausted, but relieved. They'd wanted him to stay longer, of course, but he'd pleaded various pressing engagements, for . . . he felt he'd had enough" (92). Norman's only relative is his brother-in-law, Ken, husband of his late sister, with whom he cannot even converse because Ken, a driving instructor, is interested only in motor cars, which Norman happens to abhor. When Norman and Ken visit one another each feels he is conferring a favor, performing an onerous duty. Neither Letty nor Marcia has any family at all.

Friendships are also rare and unsatisfactory in the world of *Quartet in Autumn.* Edwin's closest friend is Father Gellibrand, the rector of the church he most commonly attends, but though he and Father G. meet often, they talk about "church shop—whether to order a stronger brand of incense now that the Rosa Mystica was nearly finished" (14–15), rather than about personal matters. Letty has only one friend, Marjorie, a widow living in a country cottage which Letty, after retirement, plans to share with her. Letty "had always trailed behind Marjorie" (209), who was the more aggressive and successful of the two, but early in the novel it becomes clear that Letty's willingness to accommodate herself to Marjorie has not earned much loyalty in return. The novel is hardly under way before Marjorie becomes engaged to David Lydell, an unpleasantly selfish and sybaritic clergyman nearly twenty years younger than herself, and informs Letty that the country cottage is no longer available for Letty's retirement. Following injury by insult, Marjorie suggests that Letty enter an old age home in the village where she herself will be living an active, useful life as the wife of the vicar and makes it clear that Letty's company is acceptable to her only when David is otherwise occupied. Marcia and Norman neither have, nor want, friends; unlike Letty, they are isolates by choice.

Nor, living in London, are the four coworkers able to establish the sort of stable and intimate relationships with their neighbors that might once have helped make up for other deficiencies. Letty and Norman have spent their lives in a series of bed-sitting rooms where the tenants are transients, regarded by the owners as a resource or a nuisance, rather than as a responsibility. Letty's unpleasant landlady, Miss Embrey, sells her house "with the tenants in it, quite a usual practice" (56), without consulting them beforehand and without considering how this group of decayed gentlewomen might feel about living with the new owner, the Nigerian "priest of a religious sect" (165), and his large, noisy family. Edwin and Marcia live in semidetached suburban houses, Marcia's in an up-and-coming neighborhood where the elderly residents are being displaced by prosperous young couples. Though Marcia's neighbors, fashionably named Priscilla and Nigel, try to be helpful to the odd, aging spinster next door, they have known her too short a time to understand what kind of help she might need. Edwin appears to have no contact whatsoever with *his* neighbors.

The mobility characteristic of life in a modern industrialized society is part of the problem here. Intimacy disappears and feelings fade when friends move apart. Edwin does not live near his daughter, as he might have done in an earlier era; Marjorie, too, has moved away from London and Letty; Marcia's neighbors are newcomers because her neighborhood, in the constant flux of modern life, is changing its character; Ken's only child has emigrated to New Zealand. In addition, as we saw in chapter 3, the integrating functions once performed by church and neighbors are now split up among a variety of social service agencies, each of which takes responsibility for only one aspect of an individual's life. So in the world of *Quartet in Autumn* individuals tend to be almost as completely isolated and thrown upon their own resources as they would have been if the welfare state and the helping professions did not exist. One of the entries concerning *Quartet in Autumn* in Pym's literary notebooks makes this point explicit: "The net of the welfare state and the social services was closing in around them. . . . Yet in a curious way since a net, however tightly drawn, still had holes, Letty and Marcia were to fall through it."[2]

When *Quartet in Autumn* opens, then, its four aging protagonists are living lonely lives, unable to count on others for effectual support and worried about what will happen to them as age takes a further toll of their ability to care for themselves. "Hypothermia," Norman says as he leafs through a newspaper in the office, "Another old person found dead. We want to be careful we don't get hypothermia" (6). Letty knows that she cannot expect help or even much concern from those around her, and she has made an ethic of stoic endurance and a refusal to impose upon others. "It's up to oneself, to adapt to circumstances" (80), she says characteristically when confronted with an unpleasant situation. At her retirement party, Letty is careful to remind herself that the perfunctory interest in her prospects that the other guests express means little and that she should not presume upon it. "Letty's natural modesty and politeness prevented her from telling them that she was no longer going to share a country cottage with a friend. . . . She knew that she was not a very interesting person, so she did not go into too much boring detail with the young people who enquired graciously about her future plans" (104).

Perhaps the best symbol of the degree to which community has disappeared from the world of *Quartet in Autumn* is to be found in the unwillingness of its characters to share food with one another. The many sumptuous dinner, supper, and tea parties that Pym's early novels describe so attractively, emphasizing the pleasures of society and hospitality, are here reduced to the most joyless, minimal sharing of food imaginable. Edwin makes a ritual gesture of offering Letty one of his lunchtime jelly babies, knowing "that she would refuse" (5), while Norman and Marcia share a giant-sized tin of instant coffee for reasons of economy alone. When Letty must share a restaurant table with a stranger, he hands her the menu "with a brief hostile glance" (4).

The closest thing to a stable and intimate personal relationship that Letty, Marcia, Edwin, and Norman have when *Quartet in*

Autumn opens is their relationship with one another, and insofar
as the novel can be said to have a story line, it tells how the
coworkers, especially Edwin, come to accept the responsibility
that their intimacy with one another entails. It is a story of
slight progress, rather than triumph, of tentative steps toward
human contact, rather than the achievement of true community.
And, to complicate matters further, the movement toward responsibility and unity is counterpointed by Letty's discovery
that she has the power to assert her own independence and
to take a more self-regarding line in planning the remainder
of her life.

Musing on his association with Marcia and Letty, Edwin remarks that "it's a strange relationship working with women like
that. . . . The curious intimacy of the office is very definitely
not repeated outside it" (165), and this is indeed an accurate
description of the original relation among the four colleagues.
Not very busy, they spend a good deal of time during the work
day chatting about items in the news, their jobs, and the details
of their ordinary lives. Though nothing of an intimate nature
is ever confided, it is impossible that four people could spend
so many hours together over a period of years without learning,
willy-nilly, a good deal about the way each other's minds work.
And so Edwin has fathomed the fact that there was, at one
period, some sort of strange, unacknowledged attraction between Norman and Marcia, while Letty understands that Marcia
has an odd romantic interest in Mr. Strong, the surgeon who
performed her mastectomy. Letty knows Norman so well that
she can often predict what he will say next: " 'I have a couple
of non-stick saucepans and my own omelette pan,' said Letty
hurrying over the words, for . . . she did not want to hear
about Norman's frying pan. 'Oh, I just shove everything into
a frying pan,' Norman said, as she knew he would" (185).
The other three are all dimly aware that Marcia is growing
ever more peculiar and they understand something of the
strange, but consistent way her mind works.

Initially, however, the coworkers' response to the intimacy
that has been thrust upon them by the accident of their jobs
is one of fear, rather than of acceptance, though there are differences among them in this respect. The four colleagues take
care never to meet outside the office, thus making it clear to

one another that they are not in any sense friends. After Marcia's death, Norman wonders, "If she had invited him [to her home], would things have been any different? But she never would have invited him—that was the essence of their relationship" (197). Letty, the kindest of them all, ventures a few little attentions to show Marcia that she cares about her, but accepts it calmly when Marcia rebuffs her, for she doesn't really want to know too much about Marcia's disturbing mental state. When Marcia empties her office drawer on the day of her retirement, Letty "turned aside, not wanting to see what Marcia was taking out. . . . It seemed an intrusion into Marcia's private life, something it was better not to know about" (107). So originally it is indeed a "curious intimacy," stopping at the office door, which the four share.

Edwin takes the first step toward accepting the responsibility that intimate knowledge of another person entails when Letty, her original retirement plans canceled, finds herself unable to live in the noisy establishment of her new Nigerian landlord. Understanding something of Letty's friendless state, Edwin, "perhaps seeing himself as a person wanting to help ladies," in defiance of all precedent goes "on thinking about Letty and her problem" (70) *after* he leaves the office, and takes steps to find her a room in the house of an elderly acquaintance, Mrs. Pope. Having done this, Edwin feels relieved that he has discharged his Christian duty to Letty and puts her firmly out of his mind, agreeing with Norman that it is "altogether too difficult" (107) to give her a present or take her out for a meal on the day she retires. But once Letty and Marcia are gone from the office, Edwin feels uneasily aware that the curious intimacy they have shared demands some gesture of concern. So he insists that he and Norman jointly invite the women to lunch, and the four share a meal together for the first time— an event that marks a forward step in their relationship. On this occasion Edwin is again aware of Letty's isolation, but he is not yet ready to accept the implications that her loneliness has for his own behavior. Accidentally meeting Edwin shortly afterwards at one of the many churches he frequents, "Letty had greeted him so warmly that he must have taken fright, for he had not appeared again" (143).

Marcia's death helps her surviving coworkers get past this

stalemate, for ironically it breathes new life into their relationship. Drawn by some mysterious, unacknowledged element of
attraction or concern, Norman finds himself, one evening, "accidentally" passing Marcia's house, where he sees her in the garden looking terrifyingly thin, messy, and strange. Hearing of
her upsetting appearance from Norman, Edwin decides to
" 'stroll past there one evening and see if there's anything I
can do.' But of course Edwin was not at all sure what there
would be, if anything. The idea of being able to 'do' something
for Marcia was so improbable that he had only said it to ease
his conscience a little. After all, he and Norman had worked
with her . . ." (158). So, motivated by conscience, Edwin visits
Marcia, finds her unconscious, and arranges to have her taken
to a hospital where, since she has no family, he tells the hospital
authorities that he is her next-of-kin. And in a way, of course,
he is, for there is no one closer to Marcia than Edwin, Norman,
and Letty.

The remaining three feel some guilt over the way they left
Marcia to die alone, though it is also true that they know her
well enough to be aware that there was probably little they
could have done for her. In addition to this guilt and to their
expansive relief that they are still alive, Edwin, Letty, and Norman are drawn closer together as they perform the necessary
duties that Marcia's death entails. Acknowledging in death what
in her frantic need to cling to her own autonomy she never
admitted in life—that her closest human tie was the bond with
her coworkers—Marcia has left her house to Norman. In arranging and attending her funeral, and in clearing out the contents
of her house, the three survivors overcome their intense fear
of meeting one another outside the office. "Death has done
this" (184), Letty thinks as she enters Edwin's dwelling for
the first time, on the day of Marcia's funeral.

Again the new stage in their relationship is marked by their
eating a meal together—in this case a sumptuous restaurant lunch
following Marcia's cremation. Only after Marcia's death does
it occur to Edwin "that he might give Letty a ring. At the
funeral he had got the impression that she was a bit lonely,
even living with Mrs. Pope. . . . With this idea in mind he
went to the telephone and dialled the number, but it was engaged. He decided to leave it for today and try again tomorrow

or whenever he happened to remember it" (204). And realizing
that Norman is upset over Marcia's death, Edwin decides he
"must ask him round to a meal one evening . . . give him a
chance to talk about her if he wants to. [Edwin] did not much
look forward to the prospect, but things like this had to be
done and one couldn't expect always to enjoy doing one's Christian duty" (193). Small as these gestures are, they represent a
far greater acknowledgment of responsibility toward Letty and
Norman than Edwin had previously been willing to make.

Unlike Edwin, Letty was never unaware or unwilling to admit
that when one associates with others one necessarily acquires
duties toward them. When Norman asks her what she would
do if Mrs. Pope were to fall and break a limb, and adds, "Anyway
what is one's responsibility in that kind of thing—answer me
that," Letty is at no loss for an answer. " 'Just the ordinary
responsibility of one human being towards another,' said Letty,
'I hope I should do whatever was best' " (79). Letty's problem
is somewhat different from Edwin and Norman's. Though willing to accept responsibility, she has trouble making contact.
This is partly constitutional—shy and reserved with others, she
can rarely nerve herself to act at the strategic moment. When
Letty shares a restaurant table with a stranger, the woman looks
at her, "perhaps about to venture a comment on price increases.
. . . Then, discouraged by Letty's lack of response, she lowered
her glance. . . . The moment had passed. Letty picked up her
bill. . . . For all her apparent indifference, she was not unaware
of the situation. Somebody had reached out towards her. They
could have spoken and a link might have been forged. . . .
But the other woman . . . was now bent rather low over her
macaroni au gratin. . . . Once again Letty had failed to make
contact" (4).

But even more important in producing Letty's isolation than
her shyness is the fact that as an aging, unmarried woman of
no particular distinction, she is not wanted by others for friendship and aid. Edwin initially fears Letty's loneliness and the
demands she might make on him; Marjorie prefers David Lydell's companionship when she can get it; Marcia doesn't even
answer Letty's note suggesting that they meet; and the ancient
but self-sufficient Mrs. Pope only very gradually comes to enjoy
Letty's company. Letty, in an attempt to be useful, takes up

church work, but in the church women like herself are too
plentiful for her to feel needed as an individual. Her experiences
in the church are pretty grim: "On a bitter evening in March
she joined a little group . . . shuffling round the Stations of
the Cross. . . . The knees of elderly women bent creakily at
each Station, hands had to grasp the edge of a pew to pull
the body up again. 'From pain to pain, from woe to woe . . .'
they recited" (142–43).

Many of Pym's single women know what it means to be ignored or unwanted, but none of them has this experience in
quite the painful and extreme form in which it comes to Letty.
In order to survive at all, Letty must prevent herself from thinking too much about the implications of her situation. Taking
a springtime walk with Marjorie, Letty "looked around the wood
remembering its autumn carpet of beech leaves and wondering
if it could be the kind of place to lie down in and prepare for
death when life became too much to be endured. . . . It was
not the kind of fantasy she could indulge with Marjorie or even
dwell on too much herself. Danger lay in that direction" (149–
50).

In the course of the novel, however, Letty's situation does
improve somewhat, partly as a result of the social thaw produced
by Marcia's death, partly because David Lydell deserts Marjorie
for another woman, and partly because Letty herself changes.
Letty has always tried hard to be what the world around her
says a woman ought to be: kind, accepting, passive, country-
loving, optimistic, and considerate. When Marjorie abruptly can-
cels their plan for a shared retirement, Letty takes it as a matter
of course that she will suppress her own feelings and answer
Marjorie's letter in such a way as to "ease her conscience about
the upsetting of the retirement plans" (55). Contemplating an
empty future, Letty tries to be cheerful as she considers various
unpromising alternatives, "dutifully accepting the suggested attitude towards retirement, that life was still full of possibilities"
(106).

What Letty comes finally to see is that though some of the
traditional feminine virtues—kindness, consideration, adaptabil-
ity—do come naturally to her, others go against her natural
grain, so that her pursuit of them has proved to be a trap,
preventing her from realizing even the few possibilities her situa-

tion holds. Her passivity has allowed Marjorie to abuse their friendship; her desire to assume "the suggested attitude" in all things has led her to lie to herself about her real dislike of the country, with its "dead birds and mangled rabbits and . . . cruel tongued village people" (217); her wish to look on the bright side has made her chronically unwilling to follow up her shrewdest insights into the characters of her acquaintances. Realizing that David Lydell cruises around his parish sampling the cooking—and the affection—of all its unattached women, Letty decides "that she did not particularly want to probe" (151) the unsavory motives she suspects are influencing him.

But when David jilts Marjorie, Letty finally comes to understand the ways in which her efforts to be a conventional good woman have harmed her, and she is able to change. Though she continues to treat Marjorie kindly, Letty is noncommittal when Marjorie insensitively assumes that they will now resume their original retirement plan as if David Lydell had never existed. "In the past she had always trailed behind Marjorie, when the two of them were together, but there was no reason why this should always be the pattern" (209), she thinks. When Letty tells Edwin that she is dubious about moving in with Marjorie, he feels somewhat perturbed. " 'But I thought you loved the country,' said Edwin, dismay in his tone, for surely all middle-aged or elderly women loved, or ought to love, the country?" (217). For the first time, Letty finds the courage to stand up for her own preferences, though she does so in characteristically moderate terms. "I don't think I *love* it exactly. . . . It was just that it seemed a suitable arrangement when we made it" (217). Allowing herself to probe David's character for the first time, Letty feels that though "there was something shocking in the idea of two women competing for the love of a clergyman with the lure of food and wine . . . the whole pattern slotted into place" (206). Here Letty follows a cynical, pessimistic insight to its logical conclusion for the only time in the novel.

By taking these few tentative steps away from the passivity expected of women, Letty gains some much-needed confidence. Thinking that "both Marjorie and Mrs. Pope would be waiting to know what *she* had decided to do" about a place to live, Letty experiences "a most agreeable sensation, almost a feeling of power" (217). Though that eloquent "almost" tells us that

Letty still has a long way to go before approaching the self-confidence of even the least self-confident type of man, still progress has been made. On the last page of the novel, Letty actually manages to invite Edwin and Norman to spend a day with her at Marjorie's country cottage, an audacious act of hospitality. Letty is aware that in concocting the scheme Marjorie is considering Edwin and Norman as possible successors to David and she is also aware of the unlikeliness of the whole project: "It was difficult to think of Edwin and Norman as objects of romantic speculation, and two less country-loving people could hardly be imagined. But at least it made one realise that life still held infinite possibilities for change" (218).

Obviously Letty's last remark is not completely lacking in irony. The changes that have occurred in her life have been tiny, not immense, and though possibilities, this side of the grave, are in a sense always unlimited, no very dramatic changes are likely to occur. But the qualified optimism that Letty expresses here is far more convincing than the conventionally cheery attitudes she "dutifully assumed" earlier, for it is based on her own recent experience that small, but significant, changes in character and situation never become impossible. In this respect Letty contrasts with the childishly optimistic Marjorie, whose belief in unlimited possibilities is not controlled by a sense of reality, and who therefore feels no suspicion when a man twenty years her junior proposes marriage, as well as with Marcia, whose deeply rooted obsessions made all change impossible. So in *Quartet in Autumn,* Pym suggests that though for many old age is indeed a period of mental rigidity and decline, for others it can be a time of learning and of moral growth. This contrapuntal complexity gives the novel its authority as an examination of what it means to grow old.

A Few Green Leaves

In her last novel, *A Few Green Leaves,* Pym returns to the village locale she employed in *Some Tame Gazelle* and confronts the sobering fact that the texture of rural English life has been radically transformed during the intervening period. The manor house here, once occupied by the squire of the parish, now belongs to an absentee landlord, while the working-class inhabit-

ants of the village live in a new housing estate on its fringes,
separated from the middle-class people who remain in the village
proper. In this shattered community, traditional English amuse-
ments, clothes, and food have all disappeared. Television has
become the preferred way of spending leisure time; "the box"
is now a source of values and even of instruction. Looking over
some jumble left at the rectory, a village charlady criticizes the
"woolens shrunken or felted, or the colours faded, obviously
the wrong washing powder used, insufficient attention paid to
the television commercials" (44). But natural fibers like wool
are becoming a thing of the past, as advertising convinces the
villagers that "Acrilan, Courtelle, Terylene, or Nylon" (21)
are preferable alternatives.

Under the influence of the mass media, the old-fashioned,
bland British food, which Pym's early novels describe so attractively, has disappeared. For the middle classes it has been replaced by a hodgepodge of international "gourmet" items.
Seeing a friend holding "a dish of something in her hands,"
the rector Tom Dagnall is reminded "of a 'shape,' the blanc-
mange of his childhood, but obviously it couldn't be that. People
. . . didn't eat that kind of thing in these days—it would be a
mousse" (30). And indeed it is. For the lower classes the old
cuisine has been replaced by the prepackaged convenience foods
originally eaten only by Americans: "Processed cheese and instant coffee and beefburgers and fish fingers too—most of the
people in this village live on such things" (208).

The welfare state has also helped to alter the village. Tom
Dagnall finds the tape recordings of the views of ordinary folk,
which he has been making in an attempt to rival earlier clerical
chroniclers of the local scene like à Wood, Aubrey, and Hearne,
to be "curiously disappointing" (110), by comparison with their
prototypes. "Perhaps we were all flattened out into a kind of
uniform dullness these days," he reflects, "something to do with
the welfare state and the rise of the consumer society" (110).
The last real eccentric left in the village, Miss Lickerish, dies
at the close of the novel, and the event seems to mark the
end of an era in British life. It is not surprising that, in this
ruined pastoral setting, a village woman taking a springtime
walk in the woods should mistake for "a patch of violets" an
object that actually turns out to be "no rare spring flower, or

even the humblest violet, but the discarded wrapping of a choco-
late bar" (4).

Like Pym's other late novels, *A Few Green Leaves* portrays a
world in which science is replacing literature and religion as
the preferred mode of understanding human experience. "The
doctor's surgery was full," the narrator comments wryly, while
"the rector's study was empty—never any queue there" (107).
Literary and religious approaches to life are represented in the
novel only by such aging characters as Tom Dagnall and his
friend Beatrix Howick, a professor of literature specializing in
the eighteenth- and nineteenth-century novel. And they are very
much on the defensive—Tom because he has largely lost his
influence over his parishioners, Beatrix because her daughter
Emma "tended to despise her mother's [literary] studies" (86).
"It was sometimes a grief [to Beatrix] that her daughter was
not better read in English literature with all the comfort it could
give" (165). Indeed, all the younger characters in the novel
take the expected course and commit themselves either to science or to social science: Emma and her ex-lover Graham Pettifer are anthropologists, Robbie and Tamsin Barraclough are
sociologists, Martin Shrubsole is a doctor, and his wife, Avice,
an ex–social worker. They are all newcomers to the village.
These characters tend to see the world in terms of the unpleasant
jargon, dehumanized abstractions, and crude "card-index"
(185) categories in which they have been trained. Except for
Emma, who is, as we shall see, a special case, none of them
has anything very interesting to say about the important human
subjects in which they are supposed to be experts. Pym's attitude
toward social scientists here is much less pleasant, friendly, and
amused than in *Less Than Angels.*

The effect of these changes is to divide the novel's characters
into two groups—those who are more or less satisfied with the
world of the present and those who have fled from the novelties
of the contemporary scene into a preoccupation with some aspect
of the past. The scientist characters obviously belong to the
first category, as do the ordinary villagers, who are not very
central to the novel, but who are clearly portrayed as happy
with the improved standard of living conferred on them by
the welfare state. They do not miss the church or find the doctor
an unsatisfying substitute and they positively like convenience

foods, man-made fibers, and "the box." But the older, "genteel" inhabitants of the village nearly all belong to the second group.

Tom has a passion for local history and feels that "a quick journey back into the seventeenth century by time machine . . . was the sort of holiday [he] would have liked" (121). Beatrix cherishes an often frustrated hope that, looking out her window at the village street, she will "witness the kind of events that might have taken place a hundred years ago" (90), in a Victorian novel. The old-fashioned general practitioner, Dr. Gellibrand, who doesn't like drugs and prescribes new hats to cheer up his female patients, "when women [had] not worn hats for years" (16), is never so happy as when recalling the " 'good old days' of the nineteen thirties before the introduction of the National Health Service" (243). The thirties are also the era preferred by Miss Lee, a decayed gentlewoman, who longs for the time when the squire's family still lived at the Manor and she was a friend of their impressive governess, Miss Vereker. Miss Lee's companion, Flavia Grundy, has written a historical novel set in an unspecified period, while Mrs. Raven, Dr. Shrubsole's mother-in-law, is happiest when recalling the stirring days of World War II.

Only one character tries to escape unhappiness with her current situation by fleeing through space, rather than through time. Daphne Dagnall, Tom's sister, finds that on her Grecian holidays she is able to live "entirely in the present with no memory of any kind of past" (118–19). But Daphne can live in the present in Greece only because she is never able to stay there long. Back home in England, she too begins to idealize a past era: the period when, before she moved to Birmingham to live with a friend, she kept house for her brother in the Old Rectory. The tendency of aging people to retreat into the past is a very strong one in this novel and, given Pym's reservations about the present, she by no means condemns it, though her treatment of Daphne, who longs to return to a situation in which she was quite miserable, shows Pym well aware that it can be motivated by irrational escapism.

Though the village has changed and though its older gentry are in emotional flight from these changes, it is also true that the village remains a place whose links with the past have not all been broken. Local traditions are sometimes followed, though necessarily in a modernized form. The villagers exercise their right "dating from the seventeenth century" (1) to walk in the park and woods surrounding the Manor on the Sunday after Easter, though they do bring transistor radios with them. Compared to London, or to the new towns, the village is a place in which the past can be found still alive, if not exactly well.

The central character of *A Few Green Leaves* is the young anthropologist, Emma Howick, and its central action concerns Emma's rather belated decision to reject the world of the present and to join the group of characters who are contented to live largely in the past. In order to do this she must replace her commitment to anthropology with a commitment to literature and must give up a thoroughly modern extramarital love affair with the anthropologist Graham Pettifer, who symbolizes many of the tendencies of the present day, in favor of a very old-fashioned marriage to Tom Dagnall, whose personality and preferences connect him to the past. Only because Emma is able to turn away from the contemporary world can the novel have an affirmative ending, and so this is an affirmative ending of a highly problematic sort.

At the beginning of the novel, Emma has come to the village to live in her mother's cottage and write up the results of a very standard piece of anthropological research for which she has just completed the field work: "something to do with attitudes towards almost everything you could think of in one of the new towns" (9). However, Emma seems unexcited about her work and it is soon made clear that she has come to the village to escape from the urban environment in which she has spent her adult life. "Here, in this almost idyllic setting of softly undulating landscape, mysterious woods, and ancient stone buildings, she would be able to detach herself from the harsh realities of her field notes and perhaps even find inspiration for a new and different study" (9). At first Emma thinks of changing her subject of study only slightly: "She wished she had chosen a rural setting for her fieldwork, rather than the arid new town with its too obvious problems. . . . She removed the half-finished page" on which she was writing up her results "from the typewriter and put a new one in. 'Some Observations on the Social Patterns of a West Oxfordshire Village,' she typed" (38).

For most of the novel, Emma works on this anthropological study of the village, but she works with a divided mind, uncertain about what she really wants to do. Part of Emma wants to study the village on its own terms; another part of her is well aware that she cannot continue to be an anthropologist unless she discusses the village in the standard categories and jargon of the trade. Thinking about the title she has chosen for her new project, Emma realizes she will have to delete the word "village" from it, if it is to sound properly scientific, for the term "village" is "wrong, somehow, too cozy—the jargon word 'community' would be more appropriate" (38). She uses the word *community,* but continues to think of the village as a village—which is how it thinks of itself.

As a professional anthropologist Emma knows she should assume the role of "observer . . . on the outside looking in," and refrain as much as possible from active participation in village life, even when "tempted to join in what seemed like an enjoyable occasion" (20). At first Emma, conscientiously following this view of her role, does decline to participate much in village affairs: "She . . . had been to church once, but did not intend to become a regular churchgoer yet. All in good time, when she had had a chance to study the village, to 'evaluate' whatever material she was able to collect" (9). However, it soon becomes clear that Emma finds village affairs not merely objectively interesting, but personally satisfying. She attends every possible village function not to study, but to participate— her research is merely the pretext for her presence. By the time she has been in the village a few months, Emma is attending church regularly—far more often than she would have to do to study the phenomenon of churchgoing—and has become, without fully acknowledging it, a wholehearted participant in village life.

Anthropologists ought not to participate too unreservedly in the social life they study, and therefore Emma's friend Graham Pettifer is temperamentally suited to the profession, for his interest in people is never keen enough to involve him personally in their activities or to threaten his detachment. Learning that his estranged wife and his ex-mistress have had lunch together, Graham is "more interested to know what they had eaten [than in] the situation existing between the three of them" (158).

Graham is not concerned with people as individuals, but only
as they fit into his prearranged categories. The village, with
its array of subtly varied personalities, bores him, for from a
purely anthropological point of view "it's such a well-worked
field that there'd be nothing new to say" (175). The basic categories have been worked out by other anthropologists and Graham's temperamental predilections take him no further.

But with Emma the situation is quite different. There can
be no general objection to a novelist's throwing herself into
the world she will eventually write about, and Emma enjoys
participating in village life precisely because, unlike Graham,
she has a novelist's sensibility. It isn't that Emma is uninterested
in categorizing people, but her categories are subtle and small
in scale. She notes, for example, that Tamsin Barraclough is
"still just young enough to wear Laura Ashley dresses and jumble sale clothes (the kind of thing Emma was just too old to
wear)" (39). And Emma is interested in individuals even if
they defy classification and so reveal nothing upon which a generalization can be based: "Miss Lickerish [is] the sort of person
who is difficult to classify," she writes in her notes on the village,
"A real 'character,' perhaps that was how she should be described?" (41).

In the course of the novel Emma realizes that the first few
anthropologists to study a culture may well classify most of its
important material, but that a novelist can always retell a story
dealing with the same social milieu and essentially the same
events that have been used by any number of earlier writers,
simply because the individuals involved are never exactly the
same. Concerning the breakup of Graham's marriage, Emma
reflects that "it might have been better if [she] had been a
novelist. . . . There might even have been material in his story
that she could use, but a sociological survey of modern marriage,
under whatever title you gave it, would find the whole affair
very commonplace and predictable" (37). Emma has a novelist's
eye for the tiny, but significant detail. In the very first scene
of the novel, Emma gazes at the "blank windows" of the manor
house in whose grounds she is walking and longs "for some
intimate detail to manifest itself, even if it were only some small
domestic note like a scrap of washing hanging out somewhere"
(3). After lunching with Emma, Graham's estranged wife, Clau-

dia, suggests that they divide the bill evenly, on the grounds that "after all we did have the same" (153). Emma's immediate mental response—"you had the baklava and I didn't" (153)—shows her quite aware of the way Claudia's trivial dishonesty reveals her character.

If Emma has the sensibility of a novelist, it is not, however, the sensibility of just any writer of fiction, but that of a novelist like Barbara Pym herself. Clearly Emma is not interested in big events or dramatic conflicts, but rather in the superficially dull lives of the villagers, the weak coffee served at their charity parties, and the question of who will do the church brasses this week—Pym's own material in short. Many of the novel's most revealing details are seen through Emma's eyes and as a spectator of village life she becomes increasingly a spokeswoman for the author as the novel progresses. But where *Less Than Angels* suggested that an anthropological approach to life could help one see the significance of small details, *A Few Green Leaves* suggests that in order to speak for the author, Emma must stop thinking in terms of anthropological categories and must also renounce jargon in favor of a modest vocabulary like Pym's own. When asked by Tom Dagnall if Graham Pettifer is her relative, "Emma found herself wanting to laugh—'relative' was the term anthropologists used in their dry accounts of 'social organization,' " and so Emma chooses to answer the question in more everyday terms: "I used to know him when I worked in London" (113). But in spite of all this Emma has no more than the most fleeting thoughts of writing fiction—which she sees as trivial and unscientific—until the very close of the novel.

It is not merely in her work that Emma, during the early portions of *A Few Green Leaves,* shows herself a follower of modern ways. In love, too, Emma initially does exactly what the contemporary world expects her to do. She is interested in a man of her own age and sort of background, a colleague with whom she has "the work experience in common" (163) and whose perspective on life is unlikely to challenge hers in any radical way. Further, he is a married man, estranged from a wife who "doesn't understand him"—and who, ironically, could be a more conventional choice than this for a thoroughly modern love affair? The up-to-date characters, though some of them *are* married, clearly see marriage as a rather outmoded institution. Only Emma's mother, Beatrix, with her interest in the Victorian novel, thinks that it would be more satisfactory if Emma were "married and the mother of fine children." Even old-fashioned Beatrix, however, feels she must add to this the modern proviso, "or even not married, but still the mother of fine children" (126). Emma sometimes thinks about love, but never considers the possibility that she might marry.

There is an irony concerning Emma's relationship with Graham that is very similar to the irony surrounding her choice of anthropology as a profession. In terms of the kind of life she has chosen to lead, Graham is the obvious candidate for Emma's amorous attentions, and so Emma, during most of the novel, fails to realize that she finds him an unbearable person. Although Emma is dimly aware that Graham is an egotist, a typical male exploiter of women, and a bore who prefers "arid academic chat" (174) to any other form of conversation, she continues to pursue the relationship because it seems so suitable. She asks herself repeatedly whether she really wants Graham as a lover, but never answers with the resounding "no" that is clearly the correct response.

Just as she fails to see that writing fiction would be more attractive to her than writing anthropological studies, so Emma also overlooks the fact that there is a man in the village whom she prefers to Graham. The main reasons that Emma simply ignores Tom Dagnall as a candidate for her affection are categorical—he isn't the kind of man she expects to find interesting or exciting. A generation older than herself, a clergyman, a widower, a man whose only strong passion is his love for local history and who spends much of his time in a rather comic search for the site of a deserted medieval village, Tom is firmly connected in Emma's mind with the past and with an approach to life that she feels she has transcended. So automatic and complete is Emma's rejection of the idea that a man like Tom could be considered eligible, that she fails even to notice how handsome he is until a friend points this out to her. "He certainly *was* good looking" (124), she thinks afterwards with some surprise.

But as Emma is attracted to the writing of fiction without realizing it, so too she is subconsciously attracted to Tom. Clearly he is one of the reasons that she begins attending church regularly and develops a feeling for the service that she lacked at the opening of the novel. At Miss Lickerish's funeral, Emma experiences "a feeling almost of emotion" (231) when Tom enters with the coffin. But though she correctly attributes this emotion to "the beautiful words of the burial service and how well Tom looked and spoke them" (231), she fails to realize that a significant change in her outlook must have occurred for her to be able to appreciate these things. Indeed, she even convinces herself that she has attended the funeral only because it is "essential for her village 'research' " (230), and not to see Tom, to enjoy the comforts of religion, or to participate in the life of the village.

But it isn't only in her churchgoing that Emma's feeling for Tom appears. At social gatherings they seek each other out and have a nice time together, unless Tom's unconscious jealousy of Graham interferes. Their eyes meet in mutual sympathy or amusement. They both prefer a drink to a cup of tea after dinner and they are both interested in local history. And Tom, as a clerical diarist, shows an interest in the same sort of small detail that Emma, as a potential novelist, notices. "My sister Daphne made a gooseberry tart and told me that she was going to live on the outskirts of Birmingham" (137), he writes in his diary. On one occasion, Emma meets Tom just after parting from the annoying Graham and as they talk together "the tension and irritation seemed to go out of the evening" (178). Finally Emma does see that Tom is a good man, " 'nice,' agreeable, sympathetic, however you liked to put it" (124), a complete contrast to Graham's moral mediocrity. But of course in the early sections of the book Emma, like the modern world that has formed her, is not as interested as she should be in the moral dimensions of personality. Emma must learn to see Tom and Graham as individuals and moral agents—and not in terms of such categories as age, profession, prestige, and so forth—before she can understand her feelings about them.

In order to stress the fact that Emma must begin to use her literary sensibility before her life can take a turn for the better, Pym has based the plot of *A Few Green Leaves* upon a literary model, Jane Austen's *Emma*. The point of this literary borrowing may well reside in its very audacity. Could Emma Howick see the clear relationship between her own situation and Emma

Woodhouse's, she would not make the mistakes she does—the very same mistakes that her predecessor made. But she does not see it and so she is doomed to relive a modernized version of the earlier story. The use of *Emma* as a model for *A Few Green Leaves* permits Pym to make two points about literature: first, that it teaches us about individual people in a way that social science cannot rival, and second, that its material is forever new, no matter how many times it has been "done" before. "There may be an unlimited number of things that can happen to a person, but there are only a few twists to the man-woman story" (120), Emma thinks at one point, and in *A Few Green Leaves* Pym sets herself the demanding task of retelling the "man-woman story" of what is arguably the greatest novel ever written in English: the tale of a young woman who thinks she loves the socially suitable candidate for her affection, but who finally discovers that she really loves an older man whose virtue is his greatest attraction. By doing this, she demonstrates the power of fiction to rejuvenate the oldest, and the most familiar, material.

Beatrix Howick named her daughter after Emma Woodhouse "perhaps with the hope that some of the qualities possessed by the heroine of the novel might be perpetuated" (8). But for most of her novel, Jane Austen stresses Emma's faults more than her unquestionable virtues, and, ironically, her predecessor's faults do turn out to be perpetuated in Emma Howick. Emma Woodhouse's arrogant belief that she can understand the secret feelings of others, can manage their destinies, and yet retain her own emotional detachment, becomes Emma Howick's equally arrogant idea that, as an anthropologist, she can study others without becoming involved in their lives. But finally both are able to move closer to traditional standards of Christian virtue—the first Emma by learning humility, the second by appreciating the moral qualities Tom embodies—because, beneath their faults, they are essentially good-hearted and intelligent. So Emma Howick does ultimately fulfill her mother's wish that Emma's virtues should be preserved, though not quite in the way that her mother had in mind.

A Few Green Leaves is linked to *Emma* in other ways as well. Emma herself clearly knows the book, for as she prepares a boiled egg, she remembers accurately that "Mr. Woodhouse in that novel about her namesake had claimed that it was not unwholesome" (82). Tom's knowledge of the novel is proved by his allusions to Jane Fairfax's pianoforte and to Mrs. Elton's disparaging remarks about Birmingham. But in spite of his familiarity with *Emma,* Tom doesn't see that his unacknowledged love for the later Emma and the unconscious jealousy, manifested as dislike, that he feels for Graham, are very similar to Mr. Knightley's emotions toward the earlier Emma and her supposed lover Frank Churchill. Matchmaking is important in both novels: the mother-figures Beatrix and Mrs. Weston both try to match the Emma in question with the obvious male candidates, Graham and Frank Churchill. Both fail. Courtships that go unnoticed by the courted party also occur in both books: Emma Woodhouse fails to notice Mr. Elton's designs on her, and Tom doesn't see that there are two middle-aged ladies who are very interested in him. Finally, both novels include comic characters who try to deprive others of food, for their own good. Mr. Woodhouse is unable to believe that anything that doesn't suit his own weak stomach can be delicious and digestible for others, and so he forces his guests to practice "unwilling self-denial,"[3] as he returns dishes to the kitchen or distributes only tiny helpings. Dr. Martin Shrubsole, devoted to the latest scientific theories about diet, has, with equal tyranny, made his mother-in-law's life a purgatory of saccharine, margarine, and whole wheat bread.

A Few Green Leaves thus parallels *Emma* closely in many ways, but there is also one point it might have borrowed from *Mansfield Park.* Both novels use a house as a symbol of English traditions, make the question of whether this house will fall into modernizing hands an important one, and award the house, finally, to characters who adhere to the old ways and embody the virtues of tranquillity and modesty. The competition for control of Mansfield Park is paralleled in *A Few Green Leaves* by the question of who will live in the Old Rectory, a large and beautiful gray stone building of considerable antiquity, which lacks central heating and a number of bathrooms proportional to its size. Tom Dagnall lives there unaware of the chill, unthinkingly assuming that it is appropriate for a rector to live in a rectory, finding the idea that the house is too big for him "a rather suburban concept" (185). But the house is coveted by Dr.

Shrubsole and his wife, who see "The Old Rectory" as a "highly
suitable address for a rising young physician" (183), and who
plan to install up-to-date heating and bathrooms galore.

Martin Shrubsole embodies the banality of evil, which can
exist even in a "kindly" (5) and well-meaning person who isn't
too bright and who is trying to live by warped standards of
action and judgment. Cut off from the truths of Christianity,
Martin "seldom [comes] to church" (7), and grows extremely
angry when a terminally ill patient asks him if he believes in
life after death—simply because he cannot bear to contemplate
his own inevitable demise. Believing in scientific training, Martin
is certain that he understands others and tyrannizes over them
without hesitation. But his crude "prearranged categories"
(209)—"frustrated lesbian" (17), "in need of psychiatric help"
(224)—rarely fit the individuals he places in them. The parallel
with Mr. Woodhouse, domineering and completely isolated
from reality in spite of all his basic kindness, is not a flattering
one. Science as he understands it has had a bad effect on Martin's
moral character, but because of the high esteem in which the
modern world holds science, it has won him respect, wealth,
and influence, partly at the expense of clergymen like Tom.
The reader can only hope that Martin won't wrest from Tom
control of the Old Rectory as well, for in this world of overas-
sured "experts," Tom's Christian humility has come to have
an increased importance.

It is therefore deeply satisfying to the reader that Tom is
going to get the girl and keep the rectory in the end. Tom's
innocence in all worldly matters prevents him from noticing
that the Shrubsoles covet the rectory, even when they invite
him to dinner and hint broadly that the house is too large for
him—but Emma knows what the Shrubsoles are after and can
circumvent them. And it is Emma, rather than Tom, who finally
becomes conscious of the mutual attraction between them, which
has been so clear to the reader from the start. This occurs,
with startling abruptness, in the very last paragraph of the novel.
When Tom asks her to give a talk to the Local History Society
at some unspecified future date, Emma wonders if she will still
be in the village, for her mother has asked her to vacate the
cottage so that it can be rented "to a former student, who was
writing a novel and recovering from an unhappy love affair"

(249). Thinking of this, Emma realizes suddenly that she does not want to leave: "But this was not going to happen, for Emma was going to stay in the village herself. *She* could write a novel and even . . . embark on a love affair which need not necessarily be an unhappy one" (249–50). Emma has finally come to understand that she wants to remain permanently in the village, participating in the lives of its genteel residents who live emotionally in the past; she wants to chronicle those lives in, presumably, the sort of old-fashioned fiction dealing with the everday affairs of ordinary people written by both Austen and Pym; she wants to marry Tom and preserve the Old Rectory from central heating. Since Tom has only been prevented by diffidence from making identical plans, these events are going to happen.

Thus, *A Few Green Leaves* ends cheerfully with the prediction of a marriage and the affirmation of what is good in the social order. But since the happy conclusion is reached only because the heroine is able to reject the most significant tendencies of the modern world and to retreat into a life based on values that are becoming increasingly peripheral and obsolete, it is a positive ending of a new and puzzling sort. Through love, Tom has gained one convert—but what of all the others? And so, fittingly, Barbara Pym's writing career ends upon a paradox.

Notes and References

Chapter One

1. *World Authors, 1970–75,* ed. John Wakeman (New York: H.W. Wilson Co., 1980), s.v. "Pym, Barbara (Mary Crampton)."
2. "Finding a Voice," 8 February 1978, Papers of Barbara Pym, Bodleian Library, MS. Pym, 96:4. Hereafter the Bodleian collection will be referred to as "Papers."
3. Ibid., 6–8.
4. Ibid., 8.
5. *An Unsuitable Attachment* (London, 1982), 127. Throughout this book references to Pym's published novels will be included parenthetically in the text. Where context makes clear from which novel the quotation comes, only the page number will be given. Where this is not the case, an abbreviated title will be given along with the page number. *An Unsuitable Attachment* will be abbreviated as AUA.
6. "Finding a Voice," 9.
7. Quoted in Charles Monteith, "Publishing Larkin," *Times Literary Supplement,* 21 May 1982, 552.
8. Literary Notebook #XVIII, 1962–63, Papers, MS. Pym, 57:8.
9. Literary Notebook #XXIII, 1965–66, Papers, MS. Pym, 62:1.
10. Literary Notebook #XXXI, 1972, Papers, MS. Pym, 70:1–2.
11. "Finding a Voice," 11.
12. *Quartet in Autumn* (New York, Harper & Row, 1980), 218. Abbreviated as QA.
13. Literary Notebook #XL, 1977–78, Papers, MS. Pym, 79:14.
14. Literary Notebook #XLI, 1978–79, Papers, MS. Pym, 80:17.
15. Literary Notebook #XLII, 1979, Papers, MS. Pym, 81:20.

Chapter Two

1. *A Few Green Leaves* (New York, Harper & Row, 1981), 80. Abbreviated as AFGL.
2. *Less Than Angels* (New York, Harper & Row, 1982), 36. Abbreviated as LTA.
3. *Excellent Women* (New York, Harper & Row, 1980), 44. Abbreviated as EW.

4. *A Glass of Blessings* (New York, Harper & Row, 1981), 149. Abbreviated as AGB.

5. *Some Tame Gazelle* (London, 1950), 89. Abbreviated as STG.

6. Literary Notebook #I, 1948–49, Papers, MS. Pym, 40:1.

7. *Jane and Prudence* (London, 1953), 102. Abbreviated as JP.

8. *The Sweet Dove Died* (New York, Harper & Row, 1980), 44.

9. *No Fond Return of Love* (London, 1961), 210.

Chapter Three

1. Draft of a novel beginning "What jewels shall you be wearing tonight, Mother?" Papers, MS. Pym, 22.

2. "Finding a Voice," 9.

3. Literary Notebook #I, 1948–49, Papers, MS. Pym, 40:13.

Chapter Four

1. Hazel Holt, Barbara Pym's friend and literary executor, mentioned this to me in June 1982.

2. *A Glass of Blessings,* back cover.

Chapter Five

1. Literary Notebook #XXV, 1967, Papers, MS. Pym, 64:4.

2. Literary Notebook #XXXIII, 1973–74, Papers, MS. Pym, 72:7.

3. Jane Austen, *Emma* (London: Oxford University Press, 1966), 213.

Selected Bibliography

PRIMARY SOURCES

1. Novels
Some Tame Gazelle. London: Jonathan Cape, 1950.
Excellent Women. London: Jonathan Cape, 1952.
Jane and Prudence. London: Jonathan Cape, 1953.
Less Than Angels. London: Jonathan Cape, 1955.
A Glass of Blessings. London: Jonathan Cape, 1958.
No Fond Return of Love. London: Jonathan Cape, 1961.
Quartet in Autumn. London: Macmillan, 1977.
The Sweet Dove Died. London: Macmillan, 1978.
A Few Green Leaves. London: Macmillan, 1980.
An Unsuitable Attachment. London: Macmillan, 1982.

2. Short Stories
"Across a Crowded Room." *New Yorker* 55 (16 July 1979): 34–39.

3. Autobiography
A Very Private Eye: An Autobiography in Diaries and Letters. Edited by Hazel Holt and Hilary Pym. New York: E. P. Dutton, 1984.

SECONDARY SOURCES

Brothers, Barbara. "Women Victimized by Fiction: Living and Loving in the Novels by Barbara Pym." In *Twentieth-Century Women Novelists,* edited by Thomas F. Staley, 61–80. New Jersey: Barnes & Noble, 1982. An overstated, but interesting, essay, which argues that one of Pym's main aims as a novelist was to debunk the conventions of romantic fiction.

Butler, Marilyn. "Keeping up with Jane Austen." *London Review of Books,* 6–19 May 1982, 16–17. A review of *An Unsuitable Attachment* that claims that because Pym's methods as a novelist derive from the premises of functional anthropology, she differs from

Jane Austen in presenting her characters as products of their society, lacking a "rich inner life."

Calisher, Hortense. "Enclosures: Barbara Pym." *New Criterion,* September 1982, 53–56. An unpersuasive denigration that holds that English writers of "series novels," like Angela Thirkell and E. F. Benson, and not Jane Austen, are Pym's true antecedents.

Duchene, Anne. "Brave are the Lonely." *Times Literary Supplement,* 30 September 1977, 1096. A sensible discussion of the pessimistic tone that differentiates *Quartet in Autumn* from Pym's earlier work.

Larkin, Philip. "The World of Barbara Pym." *Times Literary Supplement,* 11 March 1977, 260. An enlightening, though very brief, general appreciation.

Smith, Robert. "How Pleasant to Know Miss Pym." *Ariel* 2, no. 4 (October 1971):63–68. A condescending appreciation that stresses coziness, avoidance of emotional extremes, "photographic" realism, and limitation of subject matter as the distinguishing features of Pym's art.

Snow, Lotus. "The Trivial Round, the Common Task: Barbara Pym's Novels." *Research Studies* 48:83–93. A pleasant discussion, more descriptive than analytic, of the character types that turn up repeatedly in Pym's novels.

Index